Changed at San

by
Joe Hare with Kathi Macias

Bloomington, IN  Milton Keynes, UK

authorHOUSE

AuthorHouse™
1663 Liberty Drive, Suite 200
Bloomington, IN 47403
www.authorhouse.com
Phone: 1-800-839-8640

AuthorHouse™ UK Ltd.
500 Avebury Boulevard
Central Milton Keynes, MK9 2BE
www.authorhouse.co.uk
Phone: 08001974150

First published by AuthorHouse 2/13/2006

ISBN: 1-4259-0999-X (sc)

Printed in the United States of America
Bloomington, Indiana

This book is printed on acid-free paper.

Dedication

To my wife, Pat, and my dear family: my daughter Carol and her husband, Bill Mahoney; my daughter, Reverend Sharon Hare and her daughter, Michele.

Acknowledgments

The late Warden Lewis Nelson, whose reading and encouragement were special;

Joanne Meads, who put it all on computer;

Glenda Culemann, who typed the first draft;

The congregation of First Presbyterian Church of Concord;

The congregation of Harvest Church of Concord;

Superior Court Judges of CCCO and Alameda, who at a lunch encouraged me to put this down on paper for all to see.

Table of Contents

Introduction

Life is hard at San Quentin, for correctional officers and inmates alike. But throughout my thirty-year tenure at the prison, during which I worked with such notorious criminals as Charles Manson, Sirhan Sirhan, and George Jackson of Black Panther fame, I saw lives changed every day—some for the better, some worse. My own life is one I like to think was changed for the better as a result of my having been there.

But it's all about choices. If I learned anything during my more than a quarter of a century as a correctional officer at San Quentin, it's that choices and actions have consequences. Regardless of the difficult conditions inherent in prison life, for those who chose to take advantage of the help that was offered them, their lives almost always took a turn for the better. But for those who chose to continue in justifying and excusing the behavior that landed them in such dire circumstances, rehabilitation was minimal at best.

The changes I saw while I worked at San Quentin were not limited to people; conditions and attitudes regarding prisons in general changed as well. During my lengthy tenure as a correctional officer, I personally witnessed a major turnaround in the way inmates were viewed and treated. The entire penal system underwent enormous changes during that time period, and those changes deeply affected not only the inmates but also those who worked with them—again, some for the better, some worse.

On my very first day as a correctional officer at San Quentin, I worked the midnight until 8:00 A.M. shift, and I was assigned to the mentally disturbed convicts (now called inmates) on the hospital's third floor. From that day until I served my last ten years as a counselor in the Adjustment Center that housed many of the prison's most dangerous occupants, I continually observed as well as experienced the far-reaching effects of these changes. The fact that convicts were now called inmates and identified by name rather than just by number was a positive change. It helped establish a sense of mutual respect between the incarcerated and their overseers, as did many of the programs that were instituted during that time to aid in the inmates' rehabilitation. However, on the negative side, as the inmates' list of "rights" grew, along with their awareness of how to use those rights to manipulate the system, the percentage of inmates who chose to admit their wrongdoing and seek a better life decreased dramatically. Apparently it seemed easier and more inviting to try to find a legal loophole and get out of prison on a technicality than to face the reality of their crime and try to do something positive to change their lives for the better.

Changed at San Quentin...for Better or Worse chronicles my thirty years as a correctional officer in that notorious prison, as well as outlining many of the legal and societal changes that took place during that time period that positively—and, at times, adversely—affected life behind bars in this California penal institution. My ultimate challenge and purpose for writing this book is to point out that, although I believe crime must be punished and the innocent protected from those who would harm them, there is still hope for those who are incarcerated for even the most despicable of crimes *if they will make the right choices.*

> *"Come now, and let us reason together," says the Lord. "Though your sins are like scarlet, they shall be as white as snow; though they are red like crimson, they shall be as wool"* (Isaiah 1:18).

Chapter 1

"On-the-Job Training"

The officer at the main gate was polished, polite, and professional in his immaculately pressed uniform, addressing me as "Mr. Hare" as he gave me directions to the captain's office, stepped back, and granted me access to the heavily guarded grounds. I drove hesitantly through the now open massive double-iron gate, wondering what I was doing in such a place and reminding myself that it was only temporary—I would move on to something else as soon as possible. And then the gate clanged shut behind me. I was inside the walls of the California State Prison at San Quentin….

Little did I know, on that beautiful sunny morning, that I was about to embark on what would turn into a thirty-year career as a correctional officer at California's oldest prison, the infamous edifice known as San Quentin, home of the State's Death Row population. San Quentin, opened in 1852, is a maximum-security prison located in Marin County near San Francisco, not far from the modest home where my family and I lived at the time I first set foot in the prison. The optimum capacity at San Quentin is approximately 2,700 inmates, but it has, on occasion, housed in excess of 5,000, with a Death Row population of as many as 600 or more, although the number of Death Row inmates was much less when I began my career as a correctional officer. Today, as a result of overcrowded living conditions, racial tensions, and deadly gang rivalry, the incidences of riots, killings, and suicides have greatly increased.

Truthfully, however, I didn't know nor did I care about any of those statistics when I applied for the job; I just needed a paycheck. I had a wife and a baby girl to support, and until something better opened up, I'd opted to try my hand at working in the prison system.

But there was something else I didn't know as I entered the gates of San Quentin—*prison changes people*. As George Jackson, a Black Panther leader who was killed at San Quentin during an escape attempt in 1971 (but not before he and his cohorts brutally murdered several correctional officers and inmates), wrote in his book *Soledad Brother*, "Prison can make you or break you, but it leaves no man unchanged."[1] And that, as I would soon find out, included me.

Born to Irish immigrant parents in Newark, New Jersey, I was a first-generation American who, along with my three brothers and one sister, grew up in a close-knit family in which both parents worked to make ends meet. As a result I inherited a strong work ethic and an even stronger sense of personal responsibility.

Then, just as America was drawn into World War II, I was diagnosed with a blood clot on my brain. When my medical condition worsened, I was introduced to a renowned brain specialist named Professor Purse, who not only operated on me successfully but also had a profound influence on my life in the years to come.

Not long afterward, in Berkeley, California, I married a lovely young woman named Pat—Eileen Patricia McCormick, to be exact— who has now been my wife and closest companion for many years. We have two grown daughters, Carol and Sharon. Carol has been married to her high school sweetheart, Bill, since 1966, and Sharon, a pastor, adopted a beautiful little girl named Michele, making us very proud grandparents.

When Pat and I first married, neither of us had any idea that I would soon leave the construction field and go to work as a correctional officer in a prison, but there I was, that late summer day, just slightly more than two years after our wedding, praying for guidance as I looked for an empty space in San Quentin's parking lot, and preparing for my interview and oral exam with Lieutenant Walter Craven.

I had already taken and passed my written exam just a month earlier, as well as G.E.D. and Civil Service tests over the previous year, and this was the only remaining hurdle to be cleared to assure my employment at the prison. As I made my way to the captain's office to meet with Lieutenant Craven, I reflected on the events of the day. After breakfast and my usual morning devotional and prayer time with my wife, I had kissed her goodbye and climbed into my car for the fifty-mile drive to the Richmond/San Rafael ferry that would take me across the San Francisco Bay to my destination. As I stood on the ferry, leaning against the rail and staring at the gray outline of San Quentin Prison in the distance, my doubts seemed to grow. What was I getting myself into? Even if it was just temporary, was this really the right thing for a family man to do? Was this God's direction for my life, or just a foolish mistake on my part?

And then I was there. The ferry docked, I got back into my car, and drove off the old wooden pier, observing a sign that said "California State Prison, San Quentin, to the left." Turning accordingly, I couldn't help but notice how the sunshine highlighted the natural beauty of the rough hillside that served as a backdrop for the prison.

It was there, at Point San Quentin, that an old wood-hull sailing ship was run aground for security in 1852, serving as California's first State prison. Run by private contract at the time, the inmates were let out to work for road contractors each day, then returned to the ship at night. As the inmate population grew, however, the State decided to take over the ship, and in 1853 they used prison labor to construct the first cellblock on the site that is now San Quentin Prison.

San Quentin Village runs from the point to the main prison gate. At the time I first came to San Quentin, the village included an all-purpose store, a gas station, and a U.S. Post Office located directly outside the gate. On a clear day, Mt. Tamalpais is visible in the distance, as well as the three bridges that span the bay. At night the lights of San Francisco and Marin shine brightly. But I wasn't really thinking of the surrounding beauty of the area as I'd neared the gate on that first day. Instead I found myself wondering how many human beings had passed through that gate ahead of me, some never to leave again. Knowing that this prison housed the State's Death Row inmates, I also reviewed my feelings on capital punishment. As a Christian I felt I needed to come to a decision regarding my belief on this issue before I could apply to work there, even on a temporary basis. The conclusion I came to was that, though God can and does forgive anyone who comes to Him and asks for that forgiveness, there is still a price to be paid in this world. When the crime against society is so grave as to take another's life, then the death penalty is often the only appropriate punishment.

That having been settled in my heart, I continued on to the captain's office and my 10 A.M. meeting with Lieutenant Craven. My first observations of the Lieutenant were that he was in his early thirties, he looked distinguished in his uniform, and he was observant as we spoke. His assistant, Sergeant Marty Grouver, was quite the opposite. He was rough and gruff, growling his response to my questions. He reminded me of some of the tough old prison guards I had seen portrayed in movies, but it was obvious he took his job seriously and wanted to be sure his fellow employees did the same.

Suddenly, after about forty-five minutes, I realized the interview had come to an end and I had passed the exam when the sergeant handed me an official State shield and a cap. I tried on the cap, which fit perfectly, raised my hand, and took the oath of a California Department of Corrections officer, and was then informed that I would begin work at midnight that night, working until 8:00 A.M. with the mentally disturbed convicts (now called inmates) on the hospital's third floor.

It had all happened so quickly that I felt quite unprepared and uninformed. "Isn't there any training or indoctrination?" I asked.

Sergeant Grouver growled, "You'll learn on the job." I would soon discover just how true his statement was.

Lieutenant Craven then suggested that the sergeant take me on an extensive tour of the inner walls, which would include the count gate, sally port, receiving room, garden, the old Spanish prison or cellblock, the captain's office, the yard office, the big yard, and the North and South blocks.

The first thing my escort and I did was to pass through the front "count gate," which is the entrance all employees and inmates must clear to go in and out of the prison. We then walked a few steps and paused until a correctional officer opened the hinged metal gate in front of us and we stepped into what is known as a "sally port," an enclosure with a gate at each end, designed as a precautionary measure so that one gate won't open until the other is shut. There was a receiving room on the left, where all new inmates, known as "commitments" or "fish," were stripped, searched, showered, shaved, and given a military haircut, then dressed in prison clothing. From there they went to the Receiving Center for a six-week evaluation and possible transfer to another California prison, depending on custody and program needs. As I stood there in the sally port that first day, I never imagined that I would eventually become one of the five officer-counselors who would work with these new commitments during their immediate prison-adjustment periods. The only thing I knew then was that I had just stepped into a very foreign world, and I sure had a lot to learn.

To the right of the sally port was the visiting room, where all inmates were searched thoroughly, both before and after a visit. Entertaining visitors at San Quentin was considered a privilege, not a right, and had to be earned by good behavior, work assignment, or education programs. A privilege card, based on good behavior, not only entitled inmates to have visitors but also made it a lot easier for them to "do their time" at San Quentin.

Once through the sally port we were finally within the inner walls of the prison. Imagine my surprise when the first thing I saw as we proceeded down the walkway was a garden full of raised planters filled with colorful flowers and a lighted fish pond right in the middle. However, the steel structure over the pond contained a siren that was used to sound the start of a day, as well as to alert employees of an emergency, and it certainly reminded me that this was no ordinary garden.

Still, ordinary or not, the "Garden Beautiful," as it was commonly known, was to become very meaningful to me over the years. I recall one morning when the fog was so dense that the ferry was having problems finding the pier. It left me with an uneasy feeling until I entered the garden, looked up, and saw the sun shining through the fog, warming me to the bones. It was a reminder that I was not walking inside those walls alone. In fact, I often went there at night just to meditate and pray. It was a peaceful haven in the midst of a very difficult and dangerous world.

Just past the garden was the old Spanish prison, the original cellblock at San Quentin, built in 1853 by the inmates living on the grounded ship. At the time I started working at San Quentin that original cellblock was used to house the homosexual population, those men who chose to indulge in behavior considered a violation of the department rules. The four-story stone and concrete building had stairs at one end and a catwalk around each level, a solid steel door with two sliding bar locks, and a tiny eye-level slot for the officer on duty to make his count. A small twenty-five-watt bulb lighted the cells, though even those meager lights had to be out by 10:00 P.M. There were no toilets or running water in the cells, though each had a water bucket and a toilet bucket, both of which were emptied and refilled by each cell's occupant every morning. All work assignments for inmates in this cellblock were for the prison laundry. These inmates had their own dining room on the lower level, and a fenced yard surrounded the unit, keeping the occupants segregated from the rest of the prison population, mostly for their own protection. That unit has since been demolished and replaced with a new building called the Adjustment Center, which houses the most dangerous of San Quentin's inmates and where I eventually finished my career with the California Department of Corrections as a counselor with those very inmates, including convicted murderers Sirhan Sirhan and Charles Manson.

To the right of the garden was the old Captain's porch, a two-story building where most of the prison's inside business was conducted. Prior to my time at San Quentin, women inmates were housed on the second floor of this building.

We then passed through what is known as the "big yard," which is the main yard area within the prison walls, with security access to the cellblocks as well as the mess halls. The cellblocks—North, South, East, and West blocks—form the prison walls. Our tour ended in the North and South Blocks, one of the largest cellblocks in any prison. The hospital is attached to the South Block Rotunda in the center of the unit, which is divided into four smaller units with a total of

1,000 cells, five tiers high. B Section was one of the four sections of South Block at the time, and it was there that the criminally insane, as well as those in need of protective custody, were housed. It was also there that I would find myself assigned for my first night's duty as a correctional officer, which would begin at midnight.

Meanwhile, it was lunchtime, and Sergeant Grouver decided to use me as "lunchtime relief" for the B section officer. The officer I was to relieve handed me a huge bunch of keys, and when I asked what they were for he replied, "You'll find out if you need them." That didn't reassure me at all, so I asked what I should do if I had any trouble. "Press the buzzer beside the desk," he explained, and then added, "but it doesn't work." I looked at the keys in my hand and asked which one I should use to get out of B section. "You don't have a key for that," he answered, and then he was gone.

Holding my seemingly useless keys, I watched as wagons loaded with hot food were wheeled onto the first tier of the unit. This is where the inmates ate, but as lunch progressed I noticed that most of the inmates kept to themselves, some even eating as they walked, rather than sitting down and joining in a communal type of meal. Before long a young inmate approached me, wearing homemade paper chevrons on his shoulders and a swastika on his arm. Snapping his heels together, he raised his arm and said, "Heil Hitler." Not knowing what else to do, I returned his salute, and the young man went on his way. *So far, so good*, I thought.

When lunch was over I began to walk the length of the unit alone, trying to absorb all I could in this seemingly foreign world I had so recently entered. I could smell the disinfectant from the morning wash-down, yet the unit still looked and smelled old and musty. The cells were dark and dirty, the lighting was poor, and the toilets in the cells were rusty from the use of salt water from the bay. At the end of the unit was one shower area with twenty showerheads. It was run down, but at least it was clean. I soon learned that showers and clean clothes were a once-a-week requirement for all inmates.

My temporary duty as a relief officer in B section turned out to be at least somewhat educational. When the regular officer returned he seemed slightly more amenable to sharing information with me, maybe because he'd had lunch and was in a better mood than when he had first handed me his keys. Still, the information he gave me was sketchy at best.

Following my brief discussion with this officer, I went to the employees' snack bar for a quick lunch. Then I returned to the captain's office, where I received my first official assignment. I was to begin working on what was sometimes referred to as the "psych ward" at midnight that night. I had no idea what to expect, and it wasn't until a year later that I received my first real nugget of practical advice about working in this particular section of the prison. Dr. G. Schmidt, then chief medical officer, was the one who finally filled me in: "When you interview one of these inmates in his cell and the door is closed behind you," he advised, "you must be fully in control by keeping your eyes on the inmate's face, trying to hold eye contact, not permitting your own thoughts or eyes to wander. Then the individual will know you are in control." As far as advice goes, I suppose it was better late than never, and Dr. Schmidt's words proved helpful many times over the years to come.

But I hadn't yet heard that advice when I received my assignment at the captain's office that first day. All I knew was that I was to report for work as a California correctional officer at midnight that night. Until then, I—unlike the inmates I would be guarding—was free to leave.

And so I drove back out the prison gate, went home, and told Pat about my new job and all that I had learned in my first few hours at San Quentin—which, looking back, wasn't much. I tried to grab a little sleep before returning to the prison, and then my dear wife sent me off with a kiss and a prayer.

San Quentin, I thought as I walked out the door, *here I come!*

I reported to my assigned station on the third floor just before midnight. The officer I was to relieve was an old timer, more talkative and ready to share about the required duties than some of the others I had met so far. As we began to talk I couldn't help but notice that he had a black eye. "What happened?" I asked him, not too sure I wanted to hear the answer.

"I wasn't watching my step with one of the boys," he explained with a laugh. I laughed too—a bit nervously, I might add. Then he said matter-of-factly, "Just part of the job."

Before I knew it I was on my own. One of the first things I learned was that the "count" is one of the most important aspects of a correctional officer's job, because it was the only way to be sure that everyone was where they were supposed to be and things were under control. I also learned very quickly the importance of security, including looking into the cell and making sure everything was okay before entering.

I was curious, however, as to why my assigned inmate aide, who helped me during my initial training period, wore a towel around his neck like a scarf. When I asked he answered simply, "It comes in pretty handy, Mr. Hare," but gave me no reason. Before the night was over, however, he explained how a towel could be used to subdue an unruly inmate without causing harm. The towel would be snapped quickly around an inmate's neck, temporarily cutting off his air supply, but not long enough to cause any damage. In all my years of employment at San Quentin, I never saw an inmate aide actually employ this method, though officers were forced to do so on occasion. One of the benefits of working with an inmate aide during my training period was that I learned the importance of mutual respect and trust, often shown through tone of voice, with both inmates and other officers.

That first night at work was a long one, full of unfamiliar sights and sounds, unanswered questions, and a turmoil of emotion. By the time my first official assignment was over and I left for home at eight o'clock the next morning, I was bone-weary and my mind was swirling with all sorts of newfound information. But one thing was certain: The term "on-the-job training" had taken on a whole new meaning.

> *"Behold, I will do a new thing, now it shall spring forth; shall you not know it? I will even make a road in the wilderness and rivers in the desert"* *(Isaiah 43:19).*

Chapter 2

"Duty Calls"

My early days at San Quentin were a real learning experience for me. One of the toughest things to adjust to was seeing that stark reminder of my new place of employment, Death Row, looming in front of me. The Row stands out on top of the North block, six stories above the octagonal glass-walled gas chamber. Each time I rode the ferry to work I would look out across the bay to make sure the light above Death Row was green, signifying that all was well. If the light was red, there was a problem, one I needed to find out about before I began my daily duties.

One of my earliest memories of working at San Quentin was when I was selected to play a gun tower guard in a prison movie starring Jack Palance. It was filmed onsite at the prison, and it was pouring rain the night they filmed my part, so I was soaked to the bone by the time the filming was over. I spent the next week fighting a cold, and I never did see the movie. In fact, I can't even remember the name of it. The only part of the entire event that was memorable was the awful weather and its resulting misery.

Frisking an inmate for the first time was an equally novel experience. I had been ordered to bring an inmate from the visiting room and to search him for contraband before returning him to his cell.

"What do you mean by contraband?" I asked the sergeant.

"Anything that doesn't belong inside these walls," was his answer.

"Great," I muttered, as I headed for the visiting room. "What's that supposed to mean? Weapons? Drugs? Money?" At the time I had no idea. I have since learned that contraband includes not only the obvious items of weapons, drugs, and money, but also things like alcoholic beverages, hacksaw blades, wire—anything that might be used in an escape attempt, to harm someone, or to create a disturbance. Contraband can also include such seemingly innocuous items as chewing gum or money. Money, of course, can be used for all sorts of illegal purposes in prison, and chewing gum has actually been used to temporarily hold together cell bars that have been sawn apart in an escape attempt.

Fortunately for me, since I didn't know any of this information, the inmate I was escorting was very savvy about what to do. When we reached the area called "between gates" where the search was to take place, he stood facing me with his legs spread wide. I patted him down, and then he opened his mouth so I could peer inside. After that he offered me a look in his ears, then bent forward and ruffled his hair with both hands so I could make sure there was nothing hidden there. The next step was for him to sit down on a bench and remove his shoes and socks. I examined them and then checked his feet. We were done. I had pretended I knew what I was doing, and he had done the rest. Next time I would know what to expect, though I would never consider myself an expert at frisking inmates. They were always trying to come up with new and more clever ways to smuggle contraband, so we officers had to be on our toes at all times.

Since I worked the night shift during my probation period as a correctional officer, I usually had mess hall duty for the last hour before I got off at 8:00 A.M. The job was simple enough. Inmates were allowed to eat all they wanted, but they were not allowed to take extra meat, sandwiches, or desserts outside the mess hall. In other words, whatever they put on their plates, they were supposed to eat before they left. My station was at the end of the serving line, and I was supposed to discourage the inmates from threatening or wheedling the servers into giving them more than they could eat. I seldom encountered trouble, but one morning an inmate came toward me with a triple serving of ham on his plate. Since I took my job seriously, I ordered him to return two slices of ham.

"Keep it yourself," he growled, dumping his entire tray over me. Caught by surprise, I stood there brushing food off my uniform while the inmate moved on. Another inmate sidled up to me and whispered, "Think about it, Mr. Hare. Was it really worth the trouble?"

I took his question to heart and learned my lesson. From that point on when I saw an inmate coming through the line with extra food I simply said, "Are you really hungry enough to eat all that?" I could usually tell by the inmate's initial reaction whether or not he intended to eat everything on his plate. There were no more food dumping incidents—at least not on me—from that point on. Prison officers may think they are trained professionals who can handle any situation, but the inmates are the real pros. They spend twenty-four hours a day in prison, and they know the ropes. Once I figured that out, I learned to listen to them.

One night, just before my shift came to an end, my assignment was gun officer at breakfast time. I was paired off with an old-timer, and together we stood on the overhead mess hall gun rail, watching for any signs of trouble. The mess hall held 2,000 inmates at a time, so we needed to maintain control. The South Block ate first, and they were the rowdiest bunch. Sundays were the worst days. Inmates did not have to work on the weekends, and as a result there were fewer custody staff members on duty to maintain order. The inmates seemed to develop a rambunctious itch to turn Sunday leisure energy into mischief.

Sure enough, as my partner and I stood talking on the gun rail that Sunday morning, I was surprised and even somewhat amused when I noticed one inmate dump a tray full of food onto another inmate's head. My chuckle stopped short, however, as food trays began flying through the air. In an instant a routine breakfast had turned into a shouting, cursing, and even laughing match.

"What are we supposed to do?" I asked the old-timer at my side. I couldn't imagine how two officers could have any impact on the 2,000 inmates involved in the tumult below.

My partner grinned and pointed as he asked, "See that wall? Shoot as low as you can over their heads without hitting anyone."

I lifted my Winchester 30/30 and blasted away. The commotion stopped immediately. Inmates looked up at us and laughed, as order began to be restored. This was, I found, a bit of a game to them, and they expected our reaction. No one was hurt, and prison life returned to normal.

As a correctional officer I quickly learned how to handle myself, as well as the inmates, in the various situations that arose in prison life. When it came to sharing helpful information or advice, however, the old-timers were like clams—one brief squirt of words and then they'd close up tight. We rookies were pretty much on our own. But as the years went by, I came to understand the old-timers' reticence and even inability to offer too much advice. It seemed almost every officer handled things differently. My method of dealing with a particular situation might be completely different from the officer next to me. I soon learned, however, that no officer laid a hand on any inmate unless he intended to "take him," which meant he planned to bring the inmate to the Duty Sergeant, forcibly if necessary.

"What would be a good reason to take an inmate?" I once asked an old-timer.

He just shrugged. "You'll know when the time comes." Advice like that was about as helpful as trying to use chopsticks to eat spaghetti, but it was the best I could get.

I have since learned some of the instances that require "taking" an inmate. For instance, if an inmate is suspected of passing contraband within the prison, an officer will approach him and ask to see his identification card, which he is required to have on his person at all times. If the inmate refuses, that is grounds for taking him. Other reasons might be to stop assaults or fights, or to deal with theft, intimidation, or any incident involving weapons.

Weapons were sometimes secretly improvised in the industrial workshops, but they were also smuggled in by visitors—relatives, friends, or even legal counsel—along with drugs or money. Guns were seldom a problem, not only because they were so difficult to conceal but also because a gunshot brought immediate apprehension and severe consequences. A homemade knife, or shiv, was another story. Silent, deadly, and easily used in a crowd, a shiv could be made of metal, wood, plastic, or even a narrow shard of glass. Like money or drugs, a small shiv was easily concealed.

On a lighter note, my first visit to the San Quentin employees' barber shop was a laughable experience, as I look back on it. At the time, however, it was not a pleasant episode in my career.

The inmate barbers are chosen to work in this minimum security assignment based on prior experience, meaning that in the "free" world they were barbers by trade. The barber shop was clean and had eight chairs, all of which were empty on my first visit. Only one inmate barber was on duty, so I sat down and requested a shave. The hot towel felt good, but soon cooled off. Another hot towel was applied, but it too grew cold. The inmate barber then applied what was supposed to be hot lather but it was cold, and I was getting irritated. When I felt the soap starting to cake on my face, I nearly got up and left the shop, but I settled down again as the inmate began to shave my face. The straight razor pulled so badly, however, that I stiffened with every short, scraping stroke.

"That's enough," I said, coming up out of the chair and wiping my face with the towel that had been around my neck. I never said a word about this event to anyone, and I never saw that barber again. But I did return to the shop and, like most other correctional officers, I soon found my own favorite barber. His name was Bob.

Bob had worked at the employees' barber shop for several years and was quite professional. He cut my hair and shaved me many times, but in all my visits I never saw him smile. He seldom talked and always looked serious, even angry, though he seemed to be waiting for me each time I showed up. In later years, when I served as a counselor in the prison, Bob was put on my caseload. I soon learned that Bob was doing a five-year-to-life sentence for robbery in the first degree. He should have been eligible for parole after seven years, but his apparent anger seemed to hold him back. After twenty-five years in San Quentin, I asked him if he was ready for parole. When he answered, "I'm ready, Mr. Hare," I prepared the Adult Authority report for the Parole Board, and Bob was released upon approved programs, which required a place to live and a job. He had a clean disciplinary record and an excellent work evaluation, and he went on to get a job in a barber shop in Concord. When I found out where Bob was working, I continued to go to him for my haircuts and shaves, as he always did an excellent job. I've lost touch with Bob over the years, but I understand he owns his own barber shop now and that he is married and has children. It does my heart good to know he has done so well.

Within one year I had completed my initial probation period as a correctional officer. My new assignment was in maintenance, second watch from 8:00 A.M. until 5:00 P.M. with weekends off, but I was none too happy about it. I would have preferred an assignment in construction, as that was my area of real interest.

Just before lunch, however, I picked up my new assignment from the captain's office and talked with my potential supervisor. When I discovered our assignment was to demolish the warden's old twin mansion, my interest in the job skyrocketed. This might be right up my alley after all.

The men who worked for me on this new assignment were designated as "minimum security" inmates because they had clean records in terms of good prison behavior, though I soon learned they were far from being angels. I had to be on guard at all times for any shenanigans they might try to pull. Some would try anything to curry special favor and avoid hard work. I had to be firm with them so they wouldn't slack off, while at the same time maintaining a gentle spirit and remembering to compliment them when they did a good job. I soon became known and respected as a hard-driving but fair-minded supervisor, and I was gratified to know that I was helping them gain some respect for themselves in the process.

My work as a correctional officer at San Quentin was interrupted by the Korean War. I had joined the Marine Corps Reserve in 1951, just prior to the outbreak of the war. When I was called to active duty, I received a leave of absence from San Quentin and was transferred to a U.S. Navy Seabees battalion. My unit was shipped to Subic Bay, where we were used for short hops into Korea during General MacArthur's surprise amphibious invasion of Inchon and the subsequent capture of the city of Seoul. I was a First-class Petty Officer in charge of a crew of carpenters. Our battalion was involved with underwater demolition, blasting mountains out of the way and clearing docks and aircraft runways.

While I was overseas I became the proud father of a second baby daughter named Sharon, born on May 13, 1952. Our first daughter, Carol, was four years old at the time. When I returned from active duty I hoped to return to carpentry work, but again the Lord had other plans. Ironically the same shortage of construction materials that followed World War II repeated itself in the aftermath of the Korean conflict, and so I returned to my job at San Quentin, where I was pleasantly surprised to find that my salary had been increased and security conditions had improved. I was placed in charge of a crew of thirty inmates and told to build a new ranch-style home for the warden on the site of the former "twin mansions" that my previous crew had demolished. It was during this period of construction work that I learned a valuable lesson about inmates, prisons, and prison breaks.

Most people, upon hearing the term "prison break," think of a dramatic and deadly event, involving gunshots, stabbings, and lots of blood. Occasionally that's the way prison breaks go down. But more often than not inmates escape from prison through cunning, planning, and just plain sneakiness.

Such was the case with an inmate named Bob (not to be confused with "Barber Bob" mentioned earlier in this chapter). I met Bob soon after returning to San Quentin following my time in Korea. Along with my thirty-man crew, I was building a new home for the warden. One of my duties was to oversee the transfer of several loads of building materials from a location within the prison walls to a location on the outside. Bob drove the truck we used to transport the materials and to load and unload the truck, all under my supervision.

Bob was a friendly, personable young man, and I enjoyed working with him. In fact, he was one of the hardest working inmates I ever encountered, always eager to do everything right. I couldn't help but like him, and I had no reason in the world to suspect that his ambition and sincerity were an act, staged for my benefit.

We finished our duties in the mid-afternoon, and Bob knew I then drove alone to a nearby town for the next load of building material. One day, in his usual cheerful manner, he asked, "May I drive you as far as the gate, Mr. Hare? I can walk back to my cellblock from there."

I saw no reason to deny his request so I agreed, and he hopped into the driver's seat. When we reached the gate he jumped out and waved good-bye as I scooted across the seat and situated myself behind the steering wheel. The gate officer waved me through, and Bob headed back to his quarters—or so I thought.

While I was gone a routine cell check showed that Bob was missing. Further inquiry showed that he had last been seen driving me to the prison gate. An urgent phone call awaited me when I pulled into the lumberyard where I was to pick up supplies.

"We have an escaped prisoner alert on the inmate who worked with you today," the San Quentin Duty Officer informed me. "Check your truck immediately."

I ran around behind the truck and looked inside. All I found was a tarpaulin—obviously the very item Bob had hidden under as I drove out of the prison gate. Since I'd made at least a dozen stops at traffic lights and stop signs on my way to town, Bob could easily have jumped out anywhere along the way.

I hurried back to the phone and told the officer what I'd found. He then ordered me to backtrack along my route and see if I could see any signs of the escapee. Meanwhile prowl cars were sent out, all local law enforcement agencies were notified, roadblocks were set up, and all vehicles crossing any of the San Francisco Bay bridges were stopped and checked. I personally spent several hours searching my route, to no avail. However, the local police picked up Bob the following day and returned him to the prison. His freedom had been short lived.

Thinking back on that day, I realize how quickly and stealthily Bob had scrambled into the back of that truck, avoiding detection by the gate officer and myself. If it hadn't been for the prison's routine cell check at 4:45 P.M. Bob might have had enough time to make good his escape and fulfill his plan. But San Quentin, like most prisons, conducts routine checks throughout the day to prevent just such a situation. This particular check was done just before the custodial officers left the prison at the end of their shift. An overall miscount of inmates in all cellblocks and other holding areas, such as the hospital, resulted in an immediate second, more specific count in order to pin down the building and tier that was missing an inmate. We then took what we called a "paddle count," which meant all inmates were ordered to stand up in their cells, holding their I.D. cards with their name, inmate number, and photograph. This procedure identified the missing inmate and initiated an immediate backtrack of the inmate's assignments and movements throughout the day to determine the area of the prison where he was last seen. The search started there and fanned outward. If it appeared the inmate might already be outside the walls, the procedures used when Bob escaped were quickly put into effect.

When Bob was returned to San Quentin, he was placed in isolation and an investigation was conducted, questioning Bob about every detail of his escape—including my involvement. Bob had been serving a five-years-to-life sentence for armed robbery and could have been considered for parole any time after seven years. At the time of his brief escape he had been in San Quentin for eight years. It now looked as if he would be there for a very long time.

I too was allowed to do some investigating of this matter, and I found that Bob had been living with a woman prior to his incarceration. He had shared about this relationship with a prison buddy who had been paroled just a few months earlier, and this former buddy had left San Quentin, looked up Bob's girlfriend, and moved in with her. When word got back to Bob, jealousy took over and he began to plot his escape. Thankfully he was recaptured before anyone was hurt over this incident.

Looking back I now see red flags that I missed because I liked Bob and thought he was a trustworthy guy. I was wrong. He had tactfully asked me questions about the delivery and route that I took when I drove the truck to town, but it seemed like everyday small talk and I didn't suspect a thing. Had a last-minute change not altered my route, Bob might have gotten away altogether. But just prior to my leaving San Quentin that day I was given a special request that sent me across the Richmond/San Rafael Bridge to Berkeley, rather than across the Golden Gate Bridge, which would have taken Bob in the direction of his former girlfriend's home. Bob jumped off the back of the truck in Berkeley, thinking he was in San Francisco. He soon realized his mistake and eventually made it to the woman's apartment, but by that time his former buddy was gone. Had my route not been changed and Bob shown up at his girlfriend's place earlier, there may very well have been some bloodshed, as Bob was carrying a gun when he was recaptured.

Though I was exonerated from any guilt in the escape, primarily because Bob clearly stated that I had no knowledge or part in it, I learned a lot about finding a balance between showing respect to inmates while at the same time keeping a wary eye out for inmates who are always planning and plotting to outwit prison personnel.

When my crew and I finished building the warden's new home I was given the interesting assignment of supervising a crew of inmates at a forestry camp near Fort Bragg, California. Since the 1940s trained crews of inmates with good records, under the supervision of California State Department of Forestry personnel, have been used to fight forest fires. These are strictly volunteer minimum-security inmates who receive a modest wage for their work. This outdoor life is healthy and invigorating, and the food is excellent. Most inmates seem to appreciate it.

Late one summer a series of fires broke out, and my crew had worked steadily on the fire lines for two months. We had just returned to our camp after fighting one roaring fire when our radio contact ordered us to stand by to be transported to another one. That's when an inmate named Bill walked up to me and said, "Mr. Hare, I can't handle another fire. If you send me out, I promise I won't be back." Under the circumstances I had no choice but to return Bill to San Quentin. The most difficult thing I had to do was put handcuffs and leg irons on him and drive him into Fort Bragg to lock him up until the officer from San Quentin could pick him up.

Fort Bragg is a small town, and when I saw the jail I was shocked. It was nothing more than an old warehouse with a steel water tank as the holding cell. At the last minute I found myself begging Bill to change his mind, but he refused. He understood that I didn't want to send him back to San Quentin and I really didn't want to leave him in such an awful place in the interim, but if he chose not to return to fight more fires, then I had no other choice. "I'm sorry you're making this decision, Bill," I told him before leaving him in that primitive holding cell where he remained for three days before the San Quentin officer came to get him.

One of the strange ironies of life is that inmates who are incarcerated in a place like San Quentin know they are in prison and subject to certain rules and regulations that severely hamper their freedom, but as a correctional officer, I too was subject to rules and regulations, some of which I didn't like or agree with but had no choice but to obey.

On one occasion during my fire-fighting days a huge blaze was burning out of control in the Yollo Bolly Mountains of California. A young man who was out of work had started the fire, and it just got away from him. One of the tragic results of that fire was that three priests, volunteers on other crews, lost their lives trying to fight it. This was my first really bad fire, and it was in very rough country, miles from any roads. The area known as Thomas Creek was assigned to a forest ranger, forty-five inmates, and me as officer-in-charge. We had two pack mules with us.

We made camp the first night, and the next morning we discovered the fire was moving in on us, closing in from behind and on both sides. The order to "move out fast" crackled over our radio. The walls of the creek were steep and it was rough going, but we made it out in time.

Five days later we were waiting on a ridge for a supply drop. I had put out my markers for the plane and was very relieved when I saw it approaching. The first drop sounded like a big bale of hay hitting the ground. It startled one of the inmates who had been taking a break, but thankfully it didn't hit him. This particular inmate was a fifty-year-old doctor serving time for performing illegal abortions. Now he was fighting fires in the remote mountains of Central California.

This period of my San Quentin employment was interesting and informative, and I came to know and respect many of the inmates who worked shoulder-to-shoulder with me. In fact, despite the inherent dangers of firefighting, it was one of the safer assignments I had during my years at San Quentin. For back inside the walls of the prison, trouble was always brewing.

> *"But those who wait on the Lord shall*
> *renew their strength; they shall mount*
> *up with wings like eagles, they shall*
> *run and not be weary, they shall walk*
> *and not faint" (Isaiah 40:31).*

Chapter 3

"Trouble Waiting to Happen"

Overcrowding, monotony, mass feeding, constant supervision, and lack of privacy are just some of the factors that fuel the "trouble-waiting-to-happen" atmosphere so prevalent in prisons. Enmities between groups simmer constantly, ready to flare at the slightest provocation. Add to that the unnatural setting of no female companionship, and the cauldron is always at the boiling point.

When I first went to work at San Quentin, homosexual activity was not much of a problem. Department of Corrections Rule D1207 stated, "Any inmate committing, soliciting or inciting others to commit any sexual or immoral act shall be subject to disciplinary action." Admittedly there was a limited amount of homosexual behavior within the prison walls at that time, but it was not approved or condoned, as it came to be in later years. When inmates were caught in that sort of behavior, they were punished.

Regardless of the circumstances, we are responsible for our own behavior. Being incarcerated does not absolve us of that responsibility. Life in prison was never meant to be a "rose garden," and corrective measures and behavior limitations are often necessary to prevent brutal physical and sexual assaults on inmates who are smaller, younger, or gentler in nature than others. Without those pre-established boundaries in place, these inmates are at the mercy of heartless predators.

Violence can break out in prison over seemingly minor issues. This is one of the reasons correctional officers don't touch an inmate unless they intend to "take him" on suspicion of possessing contraband or something equally serious. Inmates are always looking for ways to cause problems for officers, and charges of harassment or brutality are surefire ways of stirring up that sort of trouble. Refraining from touching inmates is therefore a protective measure for the officers, as well as a means of preventing violent outbreaks among the inmates, who love to hurl taunts and insults at the officers. The tension between officers and inmates is palpable and ongoing, and prison officials try to institute whatever rules are necessary to prevent physical confrontation.

During my years in the West Block, which at the time was the receiving center for all new commitments, it was called the Guidance Center. Five officers, including myself, were assigned as Custodial Counselors. We wore full uniforms and were responsible for security.

One afternoon at the end of my shift I was walking through the San Quentin "big yard," headed for the exit and home. With well over 2,000 inmates in the yard, it was packed full. As I got near the gate an inmate turned in my direction and spat. I got the whole of it on my new uniform trousers. I stopped directly under the gate tower where an officer looked down and observed the entire incident. Though I didn't say a word, there were several choice ones running through my head. The inmate, however, was already on his knees, trying to clean my pants with his handkerchief. He kept repeating, "I'm sorry, Mr. Hare. I'm so sorry." Every eye in the yard was fixed on us, and I'm so glad now that I didn't do or say anything that would have caused a problem or ruined my Christian testimony.

Finally I said to the inmate, "That's enough." I didn't recognize him so I asked for identification. He quickly gave me his card, along with another apology. I looked at him and said, "That's a filthy habit. A young man like you spitting! I will see you tomorrow."

The stage show was over. I left the prison and went home, and the inmates returned to their previous activities, though I doubt the inmate involved got much sleep that night. I told my dear wife, Pat, all about the incident over dinner, and I felt much better about it after we had talked. I didn't really think the young man spat on me intentionally, particularly when I remembered his profuse apologies. Pat and I even had a little chuckle over that part of the story, and then she said, "Leave your trousers at the cleaners. When you pick them up you'll never know the difference." She was right, of course, as she so often is.

The next morning before I left for work, as Pat and I shared our daily devotional time, I was able to say, "Thank You, Lord, for You are a gracious and forgiving God." I sang the Lord's Prayer on my way to work, and sensed the power and glory of Jesus. That afternoon I saw the inmate and told him of my decision not to file a report about the incident. The look of relief on his face was all the thanks I needed.

I learned a valuable lesson from that situation, which was never to take any action until I had time to talk it over with God (and Pat) first. Restraint had prevented any sort of violent or retaliatory incident, and I am grateful for that. Hasty reactions have caused many serious problems at San Quentin, so each incident avoided is a blessing. In addition, I soon earned the reputation of being a fair officer, supervisor, counselor, and administrator, and that reputation served me well throughout my tenure at San Quentin.

I was attacked only once during my many years in the state prison system. It happened during my assignment in the furniture factory, where I served as a foreman of special design. A young fellow, not assigned to the industries, was smoking a cigarette in a restricted area, which could have been very dangerous. I told him to put out his cigarette and then went about my business. Sometime later I noted the same young fellow talking with an inmate in my shop. He was still smoking, and he was still in a restricted area.

Now I was annoyed. I told him to leave the furniture factory immediately. He ignored my order and continued smoking and talking with the other inmate. At that point I reached out and put my hand on his arm to get his attention—a mistake on my part. He spun around and punched me on the left temple where I'd had surgery during World War II, and my temple split and began to spurt blood. My officer training was beneficial at that point, because I was still able to restrain the inmate and get him into the custody of the industry sergeant.

That evening I heard a news report by Herb Caen, the well-known San Francisco news commentator, who said, "One of Governor Brown's pets that he had commuted from death row attacked a state employee on his first day off the row. What now, Mr. Governor?"

I was later informed that the inmate who had attacked me might be returned to court with sufficient cause to reinstate the death sentence. When I talked with the inmate privately, he was all apologies and his hands were trembling. The outcome of that incident? The report was conveniently "lost," and the inmate did not return to Death Row. Though there are always exceptions, the vast majority of correctional officers really aren't the sadistic monsters the media often portrays.

At some point during this time I was graduated from the category of being a "fish." I had been around a while and had earned a degree of respect from inmates and custody staff. In turn I liked and respected most of the men that worked with me. They had to be tough to handle their jobs, but they were neither arbitrary nor cruel in their treatment of inmates. In fact, if an inmate showed signs of sincerely wanting to turn over a new leaf, almost every officer would go to bat for that man and help him out in any way possible.

A correctional officer does not have a normal eight-hour-a-day job. He must constantly keep the security of the prison foremost on his mind, alert for trash or materials that might be used for weapons, on the lookout for areas of the prison that could be an escape route, watching for inmates huddled together or whispering in corners. A day seldom goes by where an officer or staff member doesn't learn something new. Vigilance is essential—for the safety of everyone within the prison walls.

One of my clearest memories of a violent episode took place in January of 1967. I was walking through the big yard, and everything was very quiet—too quiet. It was a quiet that causes uneasiness for anyone who has walked inside the prison walls for any length of time. Something was wrong. It was just a matter of when it would erupt.

Racial tension was at an all-time high, both inside and outside the prison. Radical groups had set up loudspeakers at the main gate of the institution, and the groups' leaders would encourage the inmates to riot. The prison staff had sensed trouble for some time, particularly between the black and white inmates.

Upon my return from the South Block the noon siren had sounded for lunch. All inmates were headed for the big yard where they were supposed to form lines for the two mess halls. When I realized they weren't lining up and no one was talking, I knew we had a problem. By the time I reached the lower end of the yard I observed that the men were segregating by race. I was nearest the rear ranks of the Mexican-Americans. The whites were moving to the west side of the yard, and the blacks to the east.

My initial thought was to return to the South Block, but then I prayed, "What should I do, Lord?" My correctional training immediately came to mind: *Be in control. Never give the indication you are afraid.* I prayed again and said, "But, Lord, this is real. They're going to blow!"

Before I knew it I was moving through the heavy mob of Mexican-American inmates. No one made a sound or said a word, though many of them had known me for years. The mob seemed to open and close without effort as I moved my way through. I didn't have to push or wedge to gain entrance or make progress. I simply put one foot in front of the other, and the next thing I knew I was in front of them. This was an advantage in one way, as it put me out in the open where everyone, including the armed correctional officers, could see me. However, I was now in "no-man's land," with thousands of angry, tight-lipped faces staring at me from all directions—blacks to my right, whites to my left, and Mexican-Americans to my rear. All these figures clad in blue denim seemed innumerable. There was no way to go but forward.

The segregation of races can be very scary, and the quiet seemed to add an intense feeling of apprehension. My assignment as a counselor was to the North Block, but as I moved in that direction, the yard appeared endless. I stayed as close to the front lines of the blacks as I dared. I could hear glass being broken from the windows of the East Block, and I could see individuals wrapping pieces of that broken glass to make weapons. The wooden tables were also being broken by now, maybe for weapons or maybe just for vandalism, I wasn't sure. Then, over the intercom came the blaring order, "For all inmates, an emergency lockup!"

Those words loosed the entire mob. The cursing and shouting of racial slurs were coming from the three different camps, but they all carried one mutual desire and message: BLOOD! I was just approaching the upper end of the yard, and I had to go through the black lines to make it the rest of the way. The black inmates were so tightly packed together that I couldn't even see a sliver of light between them. Even those inmates I had known for years refused to give me eye contact, and I knew I was in trouble.

Suddenly an idea came to me, seemingly out of nowhere, but I know it was from Jesus, who was walking with me through that yard. Without a question I moved forward, straight into the mob, and just as the Mexican-American mob had opened and closed as I moved effortlessly through it, so did the group of black inmates. No one acknowledged my presence, and before I knew it I had made it through to the other side.

I saw the great double steel doors, with their tiny peep slot, just ahead of me. And then I heard a voice say, "It's Mr. Hare. Let him in!" Apparently the slot was open and someone had been watching. The door opened and I quickly slipped inside.

Almost immediately I heard more orders and directions blasted over the intercom. All employees were now off the yard. The inmates were still shouting and cursing, but not so much at each other as at the prison administration. The voice on the intercom informed the inmates that teargas would be used if they didn't return to their cells immediately. Instructions for escape were also given should the teargas canisters have to be fired.

And then the custody staff came out onto the gun walks, carrying cameras and teargas. The inmates were again given an opportunity to disperse and return to their cellblocks. When there was no response, the direction was given to use the gas. The East Block was opened so the black inmates could enter to escape the teargas. The white and Mexican-American inmates were told to go through the main yard gate to the lower yard, which was an athletic field. As soon as the gas was discharged, the inmates stampeded toward their designated areas.

The black inmates then destroyed nearly everything in the East Block. Burning and destruction were the order of the day. Staff had to move into the unit, covered only by the officers on the gun rail. The whites and Mexican-Americans were also attempting destruction in the lower yard, but had little success, though fires were lit everywhere. If any of the inmates attempted to cross over onto another turf, the correctional officers on the gun rail stopped them by directing machine-gun fire into the ground near their feet. The staff on the yard had only the protection of their batons and the cover of the gun-rail officers.

Once the groups were successfully separated and order restored, the inmates were stripped to the skin for a thorough search, and then marched back to their cellblocks with their hands behind their heads. This procedure went on throughout the night and into the next day. For thirty days the entire staff worked twelve hours a day, seven days a week. Every attempt was made to uncover the problems that had led up to this destructive event, and this eventually resulted in a complete administrative shake-up at the top levels of the prison. Mr. Louis Nelson, known as "Big Red," was appointed as warden. Many of us at San Quentin already knew him from his years on the custody staff and also from his former employment at the federal prison of Alcatraz on the San Francisco Bay.

I have no reason to place blame on anyone for that incident. I can only be thankful to God that no blood was shed in that potentially explosive incident, other than one inmate who was hit by shrapnel from a correctional officer's rifle bullet. I definitely experienced firsthand the mighty protection of my God that day, but it certainly wasn't the only time. My years of service in the Adjustment Center were filled with God's presence and blessings, as the following experiences will readily reveal.

> *Be anxious for nothing, but in*
> *everything by prayer and supplication,*
> *with thanksgiving, let your requests*
> *be made known to God; and the*
> *peace of God, which surpasses all*
> *understanding, will guard your hearts*
> *and minds through Christ Jesus*
> *(Philippians 4:6,7).*

Chapter 4

"The Adjustment Center"

When I was assigned to the Security Housing Units and my office was moved to the Adjustment Center in 1966, I knew it was exactly where God wanted me. The residents in this area of San Quentin are the hard-core inmates, considered unreceptive to treatment or general population housing. The protective custody housing is in the South Block, which is separated into four sections. The B section of South Block housed approximately 400 inmates, including the criminally insane and those who had requested protective custody for their own safety. Death Row is also part of the security housing.

The Adjustment Center was a fairly new unit at that time, and it was therefore clean and modern, an area that would usually be attractive to prison personnel. A reputation for violent occurences, however, caused much of the staff to be slow in requesting assignments to places like the Adjustment Center. As a result assignments to the center were short and numerous, with a high turnover ratio.

As I settled into my private office on my first day as a Correctional Counselor at the center, I looked out the window at the San Francisco Bay and thought about what my direct supervisor had told me. He said Warden Lou Nelson had made a special request for me to transfer to this position. I'm not sure I was excited about that, though I was a bit flattered. One thing I knew for sure, however, was that I was scared stiff—not of the inmates or the responsibilities that went with the job, but scared of the Board Reports I would be required to file. Men's lives and futures would now be in my hands, as the Parole Board would rely heavily on my reports when they made their decisions. And yet I knew God had given me a peace about this new position, so I also knew I was in the right place.

The day before accepting the position I had asked Warden Nelson, "Why do you want me in the Adjustment Center?"

"Because of your experience and your faith in God," he answered.

I was stunned and had no response.

That evening my wife asked, "Did anything happen today?"

"Yes," I replied. "I've been asked to work in the Adjustment Center."

"When did you find out about the assignment?"

I thought for a moment and then answered, "About four-thirty this afternoon."

Pat nodded. "When I was leaving work at four-thirty, something within told me, 'Joe will make a decision. Have no fear.'"

That evening we left it with the Lord and asked Him to lead us. The next morning at our six o'clock devotions we asked the Lord for guidance. On my way to work a bit later, God ministered to me all the way, comforting me with His Holy Spirit as I prayed. Upon leaving the San Rafael Bridge and entering the approach to San Quentin's main gate, I ceased praying aloud and felt as if someone were sitting directly beside me, saying, "Have no fear, for I will protect you. I will give you words to speak unto all people, for I am with you."

Just as the Gate Officer opened the gate, I knew the will of my Lord. I had the answer to my prayer. My supervisor met me on the way to my office, and I informed him of my decision.

"Are you serious?" he asked.

I saw this as an open door to tell him of my reasons for accepting this position, so I asked, "Do you want me to tell you about it, Jerry?"

When he readily agreed, I related the entire story of how I had come to the peace of my decision. When I had finished, Jerry, who is Jewish, said, "I believe this God of yours is leading you up a dark alley." I wasn't concerned about his remark, because I knew that even if I walked through the darkness of the valley of the shadow of death, my God would walk through it with me.

My assignment was immediate, which included ninety-six inmates who were probably the worst management cases in the California Department of Corrections; and forty-five condemned men, who were part of the 106 Death Row inmates at that time and who eventually had their death sentences overturned by the Supreme Court. My caseload also extended into the South Block, B Section, which housed 450 inmates and had long been known as the "Hell Hole" of the California Department of Corrections due to its hard-core inmates.

The Adjustment Center was a modern addition referred to as the A/C for maximum security housing. The structural design had four separate floors, with windows from end to end, which was very different from the cellblock. The lighting was good, and the aluminum washbasins and toilets were sanitary and easy to keep clean. The name A/C is different from segregation, or the hole or dungeon; in other words, it didn't designate punishment. The new unit was a part of the treatment objective dating back to the 1950's, a means to separate violent incorrigibles from the other inmates and offer them hope for a positive adjustment and return to the general population. That positive adjustment and return to the general population, however, must begin with the inmate himself. He must decide to make a positive adjustment or there is nothing anyone else can do for him.

I counseled with many inmates over the years who admitted they had done wrong and wanted to change their way of life. This is what I call "reality therapy." As a counselor I never pressured inmates with my beliefs, but if they asked for my advice I readily offered it, as well as sharing with them about my faith in God. When an inmate is sincere, he is usually ready to listen and recognize truth.

Fear can play a huge role in a place like San Quentin. Murders are common, as weapons are made from any conceivable source. Because San Quentin is so old, scrap and contraband are readily available, despite the prison personnel's efforts to the contrary. Some of the "decline prosecution" reasons from the District Attorney's office are based on the cost to prosecute and the lack of evidence. These decisions not to prosecute inmates for further crimes committed while already in prison can be the greatest detriment to the safety of other inmates and staff.

B Section housed a variety of inmates, mostly younger men. Many of them were locked up at their own request for protection from homosexual pressures, drug dealing, gambling debts, and most "tip" or gang affiliations, known as the Mexican Mafia, New Familia, Aryan Brothers, Black Guerrilla Family, Black Muslims, and a number of others. The Mexican Mafia and New Familia are Mexican groups at war with each other. The tips extend into the free society and are related to power or control, mostly of narcotics.

Before going any further, let me briefly describe the creeds of these prison gangs, some of which speak mainly of death.

- *The Aryan Brotherhood*: a white supremacist tip, originating from the American Nazi Party. Their main role is as hit men and dealers of death to any who attempt to withdraw from the gangs. They have teamed up with the Mexican Mafia, another source for carrying out contracts or killings.

- *The Black Guerrilla Family*: a black tip and another gang with a death code. They have a strong racial resentment toward whites. Their pledge is to kill prison staff.

- *The Black Muslims*: a group that has mellowed over the years but who still nurtures racial hatred. They have become recognized as a religious group at San Quentin with full use of the chapels.

- *The New Familia*: a tip with a creed written in the form of a poem by an inmate. The New Familia has never been one of the more aggressive groups but seems more defensive against the gang war and attacks of the Mexican Mafia. This war has currently been going on for many years and is related to dope traffic in the southern part of the West Coast of California.

- *The Mexican Mafia*: a gang whose creed is death for anyone who tries to drop out. I have found them to be vicious and bloodthirsty, with no respect for life.

As an example of this gang war, two inmates were involved in a knife fight on the main yard one day. Both had weapons, and both had stab wounds. They were referred to the District Attorney of Marin County, but a decline prosecution was returned with these reasons noted: "The constitution of the United States permits the right of any American to protect himself against known aggression. This should also apply to an inmate." Both the inmates had stated they were in fear of being attacked by the other. They were therefore referred to the Institution Disciplinary Committee and were found guilty of possession of a weapon. The maximum punishment for this offense is thirty days' loss of privileges and ten days of isolation, which is a cell status.

One of my earliest opportunities for Christian witness in the Adjustment Center was to a young Mexican named Anthony. Anthony was twenty-six and had already served six years in the California Department of Corrections for burglary, second degree and grand theft auto, running concurrently. Two years could be average for a crime of this type. Anthony was also a heroin addict with a $150-a-day habit, so crime was the only means he knew to support his addiction.

While in prison Anthony became closely associated with the Mexican Mafia and was involved in a number of assaults and stabbing deaths, though he was never indicted or prosecuted for his actions. Instead he was assigned to the first floor of the Adjustment Center with some of the toughest management cases.

In July 1973 I had my first real opportunity to tell Anthony about Jesus. We began our conversation with a discussion of his addiction and what he planned to do in the future once he got out of prison. This young man was barren of any ideas or plans beyond his addiction. Narcotics seemed to dictate his life and his fate. He had no education and no means to earn a living. My first bit of advice to him was to do something about his addiction. There were countless treatment centers available beyond the prison walls, but my first thought was of the highly successful Christian program called Teen Challenge. I was able to tell Anthony of my hope for his future as I cited the many former addicts and alcoholics I had known who had been healed by God's grace in Jesus Christ. I also told him of the work done by Teen Challenge at home and abroad with our servicemen in Viet Nam.

Anthony was all ears, so I told him of this wonderful Lord who was no respecter of any one individual over another, and that this grace was free for the asking. Again, Anthony listened intently and seemed interested, but he didn't take it any farther at that point, so we left it there. Each time I talked with Anthony through the 12 x 12-inch barred porthole-type window of his cell, I could detect a little more interest. A few months later Anthony asked to see me. He wanted to tell me he had accepted Jesus Christ as his Lord and Savior while holding the hand of a young visiting chaplain through that little port window of his cell.

Needless to say, I was thrilled, but I did ask the Lord why I wasn't permitted to bring this young fellow to God, instead of that complete stranger, a visiting chaplain neither Anthony nor I knew. I got no direct answer, but the doors soon opened for Anthony to get accepted into Teen Challenge. Anthony's mother, who was also a Christian, was very happy about this turn of events for her son. Then the problems began.

Jesus was Anthony's Lord and Savior now, meaning the gang no longer gave the orders in Anthony's life. In the past the Mexican Mafia would give orders to Anthony or other gang members to "hit" certain individuals living in the Security Housing Unit, Adjustment Center. Because Anthony was no longer willing to follow orders from the gang, they put out a contract on him.

With this hanging over his head, Anthony asked me for protective custody. I agreed. Then another problem arose. An officer making a routine search of Anthony's cell found a piece of fiberglass from a food tray. It was shaped and sharpened, even though I would describe it as a scraper rather than a stabbing instrument. To my shock the District Attorney accepted this case and obtained an indictment.

The first day Anthony went to court his attorney instructed him to plead not guilty. He did so, but upon returning to San Quentin he told me he wanted to change his plea because he said he could not

43

lie to the court or to his God. It seems he had indeed fashioned the fiberglass into a weapon months earlier, but he no longer intended to use it as such. In fact, he had forgotten he even had it. Still, in order to be completely honest he had to admit his original intentions and plead guilty to possession of a weapon.

I called Anthony's attorney, who seemed to feel there was a coercing influence behind Anthony's plea change. He refused to change Anthony's plea, and this young man was found guilty and sentenced to an additional three years to life. I testified to the District Attorney, who would have dropped the charge if the defense attorney had gone along with Anthony's request of a plea change. Because the attorney wanted a trial and wouldn't change Anthony's plea, the judge and jury had no choice.

The conviction postponed Anthony's parole to Teen Challenge, but thankfully it did not change his faith and determination to follow Jesus. The case may have had many dark clouds, but at the end of the tunnel there was now a light that would never go out.

A clear example of prison violence took place during the early part of 1975, when approximately twenty-seven inmates assigned to the North Segregation were out on the tier for an hour of exercise. The North Segregation is located to the rear of our section of Death Row. The caged area for the gun officer permitted him to cover the entire floor, which was made up of Death Row and Segregation. Only the residents of one side of the back-to-back cells were permitted out at a time. The officer noted five inmates entering a segregation cell. Once inside, two of them held a blanket over the front bars, while three inmates attacked the cell's occupant. The inmates on the tier ignored the officer's order to move from in front of the cell, thus preventing the officer from using his gun to stop the attack or from even seeing what was going on. The correctional officer was not near his phone and was reluctant to leave the immediate area to seek help. When the attack was complete, the inmates came out of the cell and, with the help of the other inmates on the tier, created enough commotion to get out of the cell area and remove their bloody clothes so they could pretend to be ignorant of the entire situation.

The gun rail officer repeatedly blew his whistle, sounding the alarm for back-up. Once again, however, the inmates on the tier refused to obey lock-up orders from the floor. Gas had to be used, but the delay caused the assault victim's condition to worsen. He had been stabbed seventeen times, and a pencil had been driven through his eye and passed through his brain. Near death, the critical inmate was finally moved to an outside hospital. A prison release soon followed, due to his condition.

The gun officer was able to identify the five inmate attackers as members of the Aryan Brothers, part of the gang's "hit team." Two of the five were found guilty of assault with intent to commit murder. The sentences were run concurrently with their existing sentence, which is considered "paper time." This meant the attackers, whose ages ranged from twenty-one to twenty-five, would serve no additional time for this brutal crime. None of them showed any remorse; in fact, they all expressed their sense of being harassed and treated unjustly.

My opportunity for counseling with these inmates has consistently been related to their misbehaviors and felony offenses committed while in San Quentin and referred to the District Attorney for prosecution. Upon review, many cases were returned to my disciplinary committee and handled as a prison rule violation. It is only by God's grace that any change for the better could ever be anticipated for any of these five young men, or others like them, who have lost all regard for human life and respect for law and moral decency.

One individual case involved a young fellow who had spent the greater part of his juvenile life in institutions for problems boys. He finally ended up in Deuel Vocational Institute in Tracy, California. During February 1974, following a riot in the Segregation Unit at Deuel, San Quentin was sent a number of the troublemakers who had caused thousands of dollars of damage. While enroute to San Quentin, these young men created a disturbance on the prison bus, at which time back-up assistance was requested from San Quentin. Once the assistance arrived, the disturbance was quelled and the bus continued on its way.

Once at San Quentin, the young inmates started trouble again as they disembarked. One officer was injured before order was restored. The lock-up of seventeen of these new inmates was in the Adjustment Center, the security housing area for such inmates. Within twelve hours of their arrival at San Quentin, word was passed by way of an informer that these individuals were carrying stabbing weapons concealed in their rectal passages. X-rays were taken of the inmates, and seven weapons, along with United States currency, were removed from their body cavities.

The District Attorney declined prosecution in all these cases. However, the means of concealing weapons and other contraband in their rectal passages became a frequent problem, necessitating additional and more thorough means for searching the inmates, and adding a demoralizing aspect to these searches. On numerous occasions, weapons and other contraband got away while hidden in rectal cavities, requiring surgery to remove them.

One young man from the Deuel Vocational Institute was a twenty-year-old Caucasian named John. His stepfather seemed concerned and wanted to help John, who was continually in some sort of trouble. His gang association was the primary contributing factor. John never told his mother he had been a member of the Aryan Brothers, one of the reasons being the creed: Death to any member who attempts to quit. John had confided to me that he wanted to be free of the gang, despite the possible consequences. I assured him that if he would give me six months "clean," good things could happen. I felt it was a positive start until one day, during an exercise period on the Adjustment Center yard, I heard two shots fired by the gun rail officer. As I proceeded to the yard, along with our Adjustment Center officers, I saw a young fellow in a sitting position, groaning in pain. It was John. To his right, about three feet away, was a metal stabbing weapon. About six feet in front of him was the intended victim, who had frozen in response to the gun rail officer's orders. I led the intended victim away, as he had no serious injury. He declined to make any statements.

John, as the attacker, was also the victim of a ricocheting bullet and was taken to the prison hospital. The examination revealed the bullet hit the pavement and then traveled around the waistband inside John's shirt. The burn was like a snake whip. The case had to be referred to the District Attorney. John had been threatened by the Aryan Brothers and thought he was making a deal to pull his last hit for the gang. My testimony was in person to the District Attorney, and I am sure it was more help to John than he realized, although I sensed he no longer felt as free to share his thoughts with me.

John was tried for weapon possession. The jury was hung, and the District Attorney made no further attempts to prosecute. The victim also refused to testify in court, for fear of retaliation. John had additional infractions with weapons possession after that incident, and continued to be considered a danger to himself and others.

Roger was another Security Housing inmate. He was thirty-one when I met him, and he went by the nickname "Pin Cushion." Roger was a Caucasian, born in Tennessee. He was first sentenced to the

California Department of Corrections on November 4, 1965, for an act of attempted sodomy. While being held in the San Joaquin County Jail, Roger considered his prime escapades as "playing around," nothing serious. Then, on April 10, 1968, Roger stabbed another inmate in retaliation for the victim's having started rumors about Roger. The victim was stabbed three times in the back and once in the chest, and received a scratch wound that ran from his ear to the center of his throat. One stab wound pierced his heart lining, though it was reported that he survived.

This seemed to be the start of an adult career of crime for Roger, all within the walls and confines of prisons. A conviction of attempted murder was later reversed and the charge dismissed. Then, upon the District Attorney's appeal of the dismissal, there came a new trial, and on September 30, 1970, Roger was convicted of attempted voluntary manslaughter. An additional charge and conviction of Murder, First, was made on December 29, 1970, while Roger was housed at a rehabilitation center in the city of San Bernardino, relative to the first trial. Again, the incident was related to sexual advances.

Roger explained this particular incident by claiming the victim had been pressuring him, which led to Roger's conning the victim into being tied to the bed so he could not get free. When Roger had the victim bound hand and foot, he then gagged him and strangled him to death with a piece of string. Roger then boasted of his killing of this individual and described him as a "fool" for going along with the trip. Roger claimed he then "covered the dude with a sheet and made him look pretty, like he was asleep." This very immature and sociopathic young man eventually claimed he was not guilty of this murder but said he wanted to receive the death sentence so he would have a better source of legal opportunity.

Roger was one of the 106 condemned men whose death sentences were commuted to life in prison on May 23, 1974. Throughout Roger's many years of imprisonment, he was a source of agitation and trouble. He was in numerous fights and was stabbed 119 times. The department ran out of institutions where Roger could be safely housed. They even sent him to a prison in New Mexico for a time, but his out-of-state stay came to an abrupt end when he was stabbed three times after only one month in residence.

I counseled with Roger when I was serving in the Adjustment Center, and he seemed to respond well. He even worked as a clerk in my office for a while, showing commendable dedication to me and the rest of the staff. However, I didn't foresee his ever being placed in the general population because of his protection needs and his attitude toward others, not to mention his general mode of trying to con and cheat his way through life.

Roger was the oldest of three siblings. His mother was a fourteen-year-old prostitute and his father a fifty-four-year-old alcoholic when Roger was born. They were never formally married, and later Roger had problems with a stepfather, which led to his being placed in foster homes and institutional settings until 1959. His first institution commitment was for burglary, followed by an escape and additional institutional commitments. Sadly, Roger's intelligence quotient was quite high, though he never had the opportunity to do anything constructive with his abilities.

My attempts to talk to Roger about Jesus produced no recognizable understanding or acceptance. He was unable to relate love to either of his parents, and was also vague in his ability to understand a love relationship between husband and wife. Instead he permitted himself to become involved in homosexual behaviors, resulting in many of his more serious problems. His expressed love for another young inmate who had been sentenced to death carried a warped, twisted meaning of love, with only one possible outcome: destruction.

My recommendations to the Adult Authority in 1976 for Roger to be given a parole in mid-1977 were initially approved. I also helped to get him placed in suitable employment, which was a boost to this young man who so desperately needed to know Jesus and to find someone to love him with a firm hand of guidance. However, my retirement came prior to Roger's release date. During that time Roger again had disciplinary problems and lost his parole date. He was then moved around to different institutions. I had one letter from him in November 1977, and then, much to my regret, we lost contact. I pray he eventually found some meaning in life and did not set Jesus aside.

There was another case, possibly more extreme than Roger's. This was a young Mexican-American man named Thomas, who was imprisoned during 1967 at the age of twenty-one. His convictions were for Rape with Force, and Grand Theft Auto, all running consecutively and carrying a sentence of three years to life and six months to ten years consecutively, with a minimum eligible parole of two years. Thomas was a first-termer and was registered under Health and Safety Code, Section 290PC, which deals with sexual behavior.

In the San Diego area one evening, Thomas had stolen a 1954 Chevrolet from a motel parking lot. The next day, while driving through the city at 7:00 A.M., he stopped to question a fourteen-year-old girl on her way to school. When Thomas got out of the car the young victim ran. Thomas caught her, threw her to the ground in a brushy area, and threatened to kill her with a knife. He accomplished an act of sexual intercourse with her and again threatened to kill her if she moved from the area. He then left the scene, at which time the victim replaced her clothing and ran to a neighboring house, screaming for assistance.

Thomas was arrested that evening when he stopped for $2 of gas, then drove off without paying for it. The attendant reported the incident to the police, who spotted the vehicle being driven recklessly and erratically on Interstate 5. The chase entailed speeds of up to 85 miles an hour. The out-of-control vehicle eventually careened off the highway and down an embankment. Thomas attempted to escape on foot but was shot in the right leg.

Thomas was later adjudged a sexual psychopath with a need for treatment as a drug addict. It was recommended that he serve a long term and receive trade training prior to parole release. A short social evaluation at the Reception Guidance Center in the California Department of Corrections in 1967 described this young man as having a negative attitude and being defensive in regard to his instant involvement. He rationalized and justified his actions, consistently avoided introspection, and seriously lacked insight.

I soon learned that Thomas came from a deprived and unstable environment, with his mother having left his father for another man. The father was in poor health, resulting in their becoming a "hard core" welfare family. Thomas resented his parents, and his hostility soon led to disciplinary problems in school. He was referred to the Youth Authority in 1960, and was soon in and out of juvenile camps for a string of sexual deviations and numerous arrests for indecent exposure and masturbating in public. Most of his victims were teenage girls. Psychiatric reports diagnosed Thomas with personality disturbance-passive/aggressive behavior. His sexual deviations were considered dangerous, but parole was approved, though none of his releases lasted longer than six months. Thomas was again adjudged a mentally disordered sex offender, not amenable to treatment, and returned for criminal court action.

Thomas became involved in narcotics in 1962, and claimed to have had a $120-a-day habit even then. Employment was sporadic and unstable, with his longest term of employment being three months. He claimed to have gotten married while in Mexico during 1967, and also claimed to have had several common-law relationships. None of these claims could be documented, nor could Thomas remember the names of any of the women involved. His plans for the future were always vague and uncertain, and he made no effort to prepare himself for anything better. The need for Protective Custody continued to hamper any positive programming.

My relationship with Thomas grew during his years of confinement in the Security Housing Unit, the Adjustment Center. My opportunity for counseling seemed limited, but he was at least somewhat open to my suggestions and hopes for his future treatment. Basically, however, the Adjustment Center had nothing to offer Thomas other than warehousing. My efforts to tell him of Jesus had little visible effect, though he did seem to react positively toward me as someone who cared for him. He was also willing to accept intensive group psychotherapy if the staff at the Vacaville Medical Center would accept him. That acceptance was finally attained after two years in the Adjustment Center.

Then, on the morning Thomas was ready to board the California Department of Corrections bus for the California Medical Facility, the Adult Authority decided on a number of special hearings for cases they considered overdue on the minimum-eligible parole date. Thomas was first on the list, with his minimum eligible parole being June 4, 1969, with a ten-year and life top, running consecutively. This meant that treatment was mandatory, and that he must serve a minimum of fourteen years. The Adult Authority member, Mrs. Rushon, only recently appointed by the new California governor, Jerry Brown, made a decision to release this sexual psychopath immediately. Her decision was based on the time factor, which was the specific reason for the special review.

I immediately voiced my objections to what I considered a very irresponsible decision. Mrs. Rushon had never even opened this inmate's central file past the first page, which noted the legal statute and time. She knew nothing of the seriousness of his problems.

"I am going to give you a RUAP," she told Thomas, meaning a Release Upon Approved Program. The approved program was that he would reside with his sister who had a number of young children and no husband. This sister, a long-time welfare recipient, would be in charge of helping Thomas find employment.

My objections to this decision were so strong that a rehearing was scheduled, which required the State to appoint an attorney to represent Thomas. Dr. Joyce Sutton, the young woman psychiatrist assigned to the Adjustment Center, was a fine young lady, but she had little experience. Still, she agreed with me and other staff members that a release was not advisable at that time, and she was somewhat instrumental in having the California Medical Facility transfer approved.

By necessity, however, a special hearing was required to handle such a disagreement in decisions. The Adult Authority member, Mrs. Rushon, claimed during the hearing that she was fully aware of the case prior to making her decision. Dr. Sutton, upon hearing Mrs. Rushon's claims, requested a counselor conduct some tests with Thomas so she could make a better decision regarding his needs. Many of our Guidance Center staff considered the ordered tests to be useless. However, the counselor, who had never met Thomas prior to the tests and knew little or nothing of his history, so influenced Dr. Sutton with his positive opinion of Thomas that the doctor completely changed her recommendation and the troubled young inmate was given an immediate release.

The results were tragic. Thomas never found any sort of employment, and he was back on narcotics almost immediately. He was quickly arrested following an incident in which he had a number of young women cornered in a Laundromat, while he threatened their lives, tried to disrobe them, and exposed himself. The length of time on the street until his return to prison as a parole violator was less than thirty days.

My relating of this case is by no means meant to degrade the California Department of Corrections, but rather to expose our top state officials who make appointments based on political need, with little concern for potential incompetence. I have the highest respect for those who serve on the Adult Authority; however, grave mistakes have been made, such as this one with Thomas. I have lost all contact with this young fellow and have no idea of his present status.

Another young man named John was serving time for burglary and assault, and he also had quite a juvenile history record with the Youth Authority. His mother had always been protective of John, even when he was wrong, leaving him unprepared to face reality. His assignment to my Protective Custody Unit was related to an inmate killing between the two Mexican tips, the New Familia and the Mexican Mafia. John had been having a homosexual affair with a high-ranking member in the New Familia and another affair with a high-ranking member of the Mexican Mafia. An eventual killing over the situation placed John on the hit list of both gangs. The Aryan Brothers were given the contract. That was when John requested protection and ended up in my area.

John was an unlikable fellow who continually used people. One day I received a phone call regarding his mother, who was in the hospital with terminal cancer and had "only days to live." I gave John the message, and he broke down and cried. As I stood in front of his cell there seemed little I could do. This man reacted like a wounded boy. I have to admit that I had no desire to touch or even pray for John, as he seemed so unclean. But then he asked, "Mr. Hare, will you pray for my mother?"

His request got my attention. My God always had His way. "John, why don't you pray?" I asked.

"I don't know how to pray, Mr. Hare."

Before I knew it I was holding John's hands and lifting the need up to our God. What I didn't know was that a group of approximately ten inmates had gathered on the tier around John's cell. The South Block B Section is a long area, and the gun guard was at the lower end. He noticed the group as it formed, but nothing came of it. Maybe they were just curious, or maybe God was touching others in His own way.

At lunchtime I met with Warden Louis Nelson. While we ate I talked to him about John's situation.

"What do you have in mind, Joe?" he asked.

"I would like to send John down to Chino, then take him to visit with his mother in the hospital." Chino is a minimum security prison in Southern California near the hospital where John's mother was dying.

"Joe, you can't do that," he told me.

"But you can, Lou," I argued.

Later that afternoon Lou called. "Joe, have your man ready for the Chino bus tomorrow morning."

John was at the hospital in two days. The Lieutenant at the Chino Institution had dressed John out in civilian clothes and did not use security irons. The young man was able to visit with his mother just hours before she died. He was back in the Adjustment Center by the weekend.

Let me give you one final illustration of my experiences with the inmates in the Adjustment Center. Inmate Johnny Spain was the who was running right behind Black Panther George Jackson when Jackson was shot and killed during his escape attempt, which I will talk about in detail in the next chapter. A few years after that incident, Johnny requested a personal interview with me at my office. I had no idea why, but I approved the request. Due to the maximum security and Johnny's potential for violence, he was shackled with handcuffs and leg irons throughout our meeting. In addition, there was a correctional officer standing directly behind Johnny holding a chain attached to the inmate. The officer remained in my office as Johnny and I talked.

I looked at the man with all his chains and security precautions and thought, *Oh Lord, what now?* God didn't need any further explanation; He had heard my call. "What's the problem, Johnny?" I asked.

The reason was slow in coming. Johnny had a letter in his hand. "Mr. Hare," he said finally, "I need your advice." He paused, and I knew he wanted me to take the letter, which I did.

"Why do you need my advice?" I asked.

"Because I know you're a Christian and you'll help me."

I felt very much at ease, even before we discussed the problem. I asked the officer if he minded waiting outside my office. He was hesitant, but after we made eye contact, he carried out my instruction.

Johnny seemed to relax then, not only physically but in his entire being.

The letter was from his mother who had not seen nor been in contact with her son for fifteen years. Now she wanted to visit him and bring his fourteen-year-old sister, whom he had not even known existed, to meet him. Johnny's mother was white, and his father was black. Johnny had been born out of wedlock. As a child he was raised by another family who was black. His mother had eventually married a white man and had a daughter with him, the half-sister Johnny's mother wanted to bring along on the visit.

Johnny felt he was neither black nor white, and it was confusing and painful for him, as was the prospect of seeing his mother again after all these years and meeting a sister he hadn't even known he had. I felt a personal pain for this man. Maybe it was because I could see him as a child who had not been wanted by either of his natural parents. I simply could not brush off this matter by telling him, "This is a personal matter, and you have to decide what to do for yourself." I truly felt my Jesus had given me a very special privilege to be entrusted with this meeting and conversation, even though I don't recall all that we discussed. I do know, however, that the family's three-way meeting eventually took place and it seemed to bring some degree of healing for all of them.

On my own I never knew exactly what I should say to these inmates, but I believe God gave me the right words from the Scriptures as I set my heart to do God's work in the Adjustment Center.

> *And the vessel that he made of clay was*
> *marred in the hand of the potter; so he*
> *made it again into another vessel, as*
> *it seemed good to the potter to make*
> *(Jeremiah 18:3).*

Chapter 5

"Up Close and Personal...with Three Infamous Inmates"

To say I met some interesting inmates during my nearly three-decade long tenure as a correctional officer/counselor at San Quentin would indeed be an understatement. If I learned anything about these inmates during those years, it was that there was a lot more to them than their often gruff exteriors or lengthy criminal records would indicate. For me it was a matter of beginning to see them as real people with real needs and emotions, hopes and dreams, aspirations and potential. Tragically, much of that potential went unrealized, not so much because these men had ended up in prison but because they were unwilling to accept or admit their own responsibility for the situations that landed them there. Consequently, true rehabilitation was minimal at best, particularly as society's attitudes toward those who committed even the most heinous of crimes began to change, and inmates spent their time and energy seeking legal loopholes to get out of serving their sentences, rather than admitting their wrong and seeking to turn their lives around. In addition, I, along with anyone else employed in the prison system, was limited in what I could say to the inmates regarding their need for a relationship with Jesus Christ. Employees were not allowed to broach the subject of religion unless the inmates initiated the conversation. Even then, we had to walk a very fine line. As a result, I learned to rely more and more on prayer to open doors and draw men's hearts, regardless of my own personal limitations.

The "Soledad Seven"

One of the most well-known and controversial inmates of all time was housed in San Quentin's Adjustment Center in 1970. His name was George Jackson, a leader of the radical Black Panthers group, and to this day the memory of the tragedy caused by this man still stirs up my emotions as few other memories can.

The Black Panthers became infamous in the 1960's, primarily due to their violent tactics, which they obviously felt were necessary in order to be heard and to receive consideration for what they considered the "rights and slights" of the black race. George Jackson, one of their prominent leaders, believed the laws of this land were applicable to the white man only, as he felt there was no justice for anyone else, particularly those of his own African-American race. The gun quickly became his weapon of choice, the symbol of his power. Jackson had a long history of violence and was serving a sentence at the Soledad State Prison in California in 1970, when he became involved in a racial disturbance and was the prime suspect in the killing of a correctional officer. The trial for the seven inmates involved in this incident—soon to be known as the "Soledad Seven"—was scheduled to be held in the Marin County Superior Court.

San Quentin is located just six miles south of this superior court, so the inmates were placed in the most secure spot in the prison, the Adjustment Center, where I worked as a counselor for many years. On August 7, 1970, the trial began for three of the seven inmates, who were then transferred by sheriff's deputies to the court. George Jackson and three of the other seven were retained at San Quentin.

In the meantime, avowed Communist Angela Davis, George Jackson's lover and ardent supporter, had come up with an escape plot for the Soledad Seven, which would take place while the trial was in progress. Angela, who mistakenly believed that all the members of the Soledad Seven would be present at the trial, rented a van and purchased the necessary weapons for the planned escape. George's seventeen-year-old brother, Jonathan, was also a willing accomplice to this daring plan. His part was to carry the weapons into the courtroom, hidden under a long trench coat. He would also be carrying a briefcase, which would help portray him as having a legitimate purpose for being there.

Angela and Jonathan drove to the superior court together and parked their rented van in the Marin Civic Center parking lot. Angela then left the scene, and Jonathan walked into the courtroom where he found an empty chair in the public seating area. Shortly after the trial was underway and the seating area was full, Jonathan stood up, held his pistol in the air, and shouted, "That is enough!" By the time the startled courtroom occupants turned their eyes toward the angry teenager, he was already moving from his seat. He quickly went to the table where two of the three inmates were seated beside their defense attorney and handed one of them—inmate McClain—his gun. Jonathan then removed a carbine from underneath his coat.

McClain, now armed, hurried to the front of the courtroom and got behind Judge Haley. Putting the gun to the judge's head he hollered, "Nobody move or I'll kill him." Inmate Magee, who was sitting in the witness stand, jumped up and ordered the court deputy to remove his handcuffs, which he did.

During this time Jonathan Jackson produced a shotgun from under his coat and dumped the contents of his briefcase—adhesive tape, coils of wire, and sticks of dynamite taped together—on the floor. He then passed the tape and the shotgun to McClain, who quickly taped the shotgun to Judge Haley's neck, with the barrel under his chin. Jonathan then tossed the sticks of dynamite on the judge's desk, turned to the jurors and, pointing the carbine in their direction, shouted, "All of you, down on the floor." The response was swift, as everyone in the room, with the exception of those who were involved in the escape attempt, dropped.

Inmate Christmas was also armed by now, and all three inmates had been freed of their restraints. Magee then opened the courtroom door, glanced out into the hallway, and pointed his gun at a young couple with a baby, ordering them to come inside. Magee also spotted a civilian male in the hallway and demanded that he give him his sports jacket. The man immediately complied and was inexplicably allowed to leave.

After that the courtroom was silent for a moment, as the question of what would happen next hung in the air. Inmate McClain answered that question when he ordered the judge to call the sheriff. Judge Haley made the call and said, "They are holding us hostage. They have guns, and they mean business. Clear the area of all security." Then McClain grabbed the phone from the judge's hand and shouted into the receiver, "And if I get killed, the judge gets killed."

The three inmates took seven other hostages besides the judge—the couple with the baby, three women jurors, and the prosecutor, Gary Thomas. With the exception of the couple with the baby, the hostages were wired around the waist with their hands secured and a wire restraint binding them together. As the three escapees and their hostages exited the courtroom into the main corridor and on to the elevator, many civilians in the area had no idea what was going on. All sheriff's deputies had been ordered to holster their sidearms and make no attempt to stop the group as it made its exit.

McClain still held a revolver in his right hand as he walked with his left hand on the trigger of the shotgun taped to Judge Haley's neck. Magee walked directly behind them, a revolver in his left hand and his right arm behind the judge. As they were leaving the main building and heading toward the parking lot, the inmateor is released the young couple with the baby, all of them unharmed. The three escapees and their remaining hostages then proceeded only a few more steps before encountering a deputy sheriff who was still armed. Magee ordered the officer to drop his shotgun and sidearm or "the judge is dead." The deputy complied, and Magee picked up the weapons and continued on with the rest of the group toward the yellow van that was waiting for them in the west parking lot.

McClain entered the van on the driver's side, with Jonathan Jackson riding "shotgun" in the front seat beside him. The remainder of the group entered the van from the rear door. Prosecutor Gary Thomas and Judge Haley sat in the seat immediately behind the driver's seat, with inmate Magee sitting next to the judge, still holding the shotgun taped to his neck and pointed under his chin on the right side of his jaw. The rest of the hostages sat in the back of the van with inmate Christmas. Angela Davis, so instrumental in arranging this escape attempt, was not with them.

The parking lot was quiet, almost deserted, as McClain started the van and backed it up from its parked position. Suddenly the van jerked to a stop, and for some unknown reason Jonathan Jackson and McClain changed places. With Jonathan driving, the van exited the parking lot and proceeded toward the south arch, leading out of the parking lot and onto a busy street.

By this time a roadblock had been established. The van stopped within thirty yards of a state vehicle. An armed correctional officer was crouched behind the rear of the car. Jonathan pointed his revolver out the driver's side window and fired a shot at the officer, who ducked and returned fire, hitting Jonathan in the right hand. As Jonathan rested his bleeding hand on the engine housing, Prosecutor Thomas glanced at the judge and was relieved to see that he was still alive. Then he heard another shot, this one closer than the last. It was Magee, pulling the trigger of the shotgun taped to Judge Haley's neck. Almost simultaneously, Thomas saw the judge's face dissolve right before his eyes.

Shocked and driven by instinct and adrenaline, Prosecutor Thomas reached over the front seat and grabbed the revolver from Jonathan, then fired at McClain, who was moving toward the left of the van to grab another loaded shotgun. McClain dropped, and Thomas fired two more shots, one at Christmas and one at Magee. The bullets found their marks, and the two men fell.

Then, just as Thomas became aware of shots being fired from outside the van, he felt a sharp pain in his back, and he collapsed. The entire shooting incident had lasted only nineteen seconds. When the smoke cleared, Judge Haley was dead, as was Jonathan Jackson and inmates McClain and Christmas. McGee survived his wound to the chest, and was returned to San Quentin to await another trial, this time with additional charges resulting from the escape attempt. One woman juror was wounded, but survived. Gary Thomas, the brave prosecutor whose clear thinking and quick actions prevented what surely would have been further carnage, recovered from his gunshot wound but was paralyzed from the waist down and has been confined to a wheelchair ever since.

Angela Davis, though not physically present during the kidnapping and attempted escape in the van, was arrested when an investigation proved that she had rented the van and obtained the weapons that were used in the botched attempt, and also had accompanied Jonathan Jackson on his drive to the superior court that day. However, Davis' claim of innocence was heard by a Presbyterian church in Marin County; misguided compassion and the mistaken belief that she couldn't receive a fair trial moved the small congregation to request a contribution of $10,000 from their Presbytery to assist in Ms. Davis' legal defense. Soon, however, the resulting controversy among Presbyterians throughout the country resulted in the recall of the contribution. Davis was subsequently tried and acquitted. She has since made her living speaking in various venues, particularly the college and university campuses of America. Jonathan Jackson's family filed a lawsuit against the State of California, but it was denied.

Meanwhile, the remaining four members of the Soledad Seven, including George Jackson, were still housed in the maximum-security section of San Quentin prison, awaiting their own trial. Slightly over one year after the tragic escape attempt at the courthouse, at 10:15 A.M. on August 21, 1971—my day off, by the way—two individuals signed in separately to see Jackson. One was an attorney named Stephen Bingham, and the other was a legal investigator named Vanetta Anderson. Though they arrived at the same time and requested to see the same inmate, they did not give any indication that they were together or even knew one another.

After passing through the main gate, the two were directed to an inner gate known as the inspectascope, which is similar to the gates set up in airports today to detect any metal objects that might be hidden on the person passing through. Correctional officer Bernard Betts was on duty when Attorney Bingham was passed through the gate at 10:20 A.M., bringing nothing in with him. Ms. Anderson, however, was carrying what appeared to be a portable typewriter case. When Betts opened it for inspection he found a thick sheaf of legal papers and a tape recorder. He removed the back of the recorder and noted four C batteries, the usual components, and a speaker. What he couldn't see was a three-inch hidden area inside the recorder. Since all seemed well, he passed the legal investigator through with her case and its contents.

By early afternoon Officer Betts noted that Anderson and Bingham were chatting together in the visiting area. In addition, the attorney was back and forth using the public telephone. This was enough to concern Betts, so he called Lieutenant Daniel Scarborough in the visiting room. Scarborough then told Betts that, due to two separate institution rules, he had denied both Anderson and Bingham permission to visit with Jackson. It seems that Anderson had just visited Jackson three days earlier, and the rules stated that she could visit him only once each week. Attorney Bingham, on the other hand, had failed to call ahead to schedule his visit, a requirement for inmates in high security housing. But the two continued to wait around despite the denial of their visits, while Bingham argued that the visit was necessary because it was related to the prior charges against Jackson for the killing of the Soledad correctional officer. The trial was pending, and Bingham insisted he needed to meet with his client.

About 11:15 A.M. the attorney received a special clearance for the visit from then associate warden, James Parkes. The call finally came through to Sergeant McCray at the Adjustment Center at 1:00 P.M., informing him that Jackson's attorney was waiting to see him in the visiting room.

At the visiting room desk Lieutenant Scarborough asked Bingham if he had a tape recorder with him. Bingham said he did not. At that point Vanetta Anderson, who was standing nearby, volunteered her own tape recorder, which the attorney gratefully accepted after it was approved by the lieutenant. Inmate Jackson was now out of his cell and in the Adjustment Center foyer, going through a skin search. He was stripped and his body examined, as well as his clothes and the belongings he was taking with him on his visit with his attorney. The gun rail officers were alerted, and two escort officers delivered Jackson to the visiting room, where he was again searched prior to entering the maximum security visiting room with his attorney. Then the door was secured behind him.

Shortly after the visit commenced, Bingham was let out of the room to get some papers he had left in the main visiting room, possibly in the care of Vanetta Anderson. He soon returned to complete the visit, which ended at 2:20 P.M. Although Anderson had not been permitted into the visiting room with Jackson at any time, she lingered in the visiting area until Jackson's attorney completed his visit, and then they left together, checking out of the main gate at the same time.

Lieutenant Scarborough then called for the escort officer, Frank DeLeon, to return Jackson to the Adjustment Center. Once there, Officer Urbana Rubiaca spotted something shiny in Jackson's hair, so the inmate was ordered to ruffle his hair. To the shock of the four officers present—Rubiaca, DeLeon, Paul Criscus, and Sergeant McCray—Jackson instead reached up and jerked off a wig that looked remarkably like his own "Afro" hairstyle, grabbed an automatic pistol that had been concealed beneath the wig, and calmly announced, "All right, gentlemen, the Black Dragon has come."

Jackson then ordered Officers DeLeon, Criscus, and McCray down onto the floor before turning the gun on Officer Rubiaca and demanding that he open the cells. When Rubiaca responded that he did not have the key, Jackson whirled on McCray and sneered, "You. Open the bar and the gate."

The bar is operated from an enclosed metal structure, and has an electronic system that controls the entire cell security. The key is normally in the possession of the unit sergeant, and that was McCray.

He had no choice but to comply with Jackson's order. As soon as the cells were opened, ten to fifteen inmates associated with the Black Panthers, along with other inmates who had joined them, poured in from the north side of the first floor. They quickly covered the officers' heads with pillowcases, then bound them hand and foot with electric cords from a cell radio. As everyone else watched, officers Kasner and Criscus were beaten and their throats slashed, and then they were thrown into an empty cell and left for dead. Officer DeLeon was then beaten and strangled to death, and thrown into the cell with the first two officers.

While the slaughter continued in the Adjustment Center, an officer named Breckenridge was escorting another inmate, John Clitchet, from the visiting room back to his cell. The yard office was cleared to pass the escort and inmate to the Adjustment Center. With no idea of what was going on inside, the officer unlocked the door and stepped in with inmate Clitchet. Officer Breckenridge was immediately grabbed by one of the inmates. Breckenridge and Rubiaca were then bound hand and foot like the others had been, their throats were slashed, and they were thrown into the cell with the rest of the bodies.

The time was now 3:00 P.M., and Sergeant Graham, the escort sergeant, began to get concerned about the lengthy delay of his officer's return, so he decided to check and make sure everything was all right. He proceeded to the yard office and received clearance for the Adjustment Center, but he had no sooner entered the center than he too was grabbed by an inmate. Graham was then taken to the cell where the other victims lay in a pool of their own blood, and then he was shot by Jackson and dumped on top of the others.

Alerted by the shots, the yard officer, Carl Adams, gave the alarm to the gun posts in the area. Officer Adams then looked through the

Adjustment Center front door window and saw Jackson armed with a gun and apparently in charge of what was going on inside. John Frank, the gun rail officer who had just been going off duty when he also heard the shots, ran toward the west corner of the north block and dropped to his stomach so he could have a clear view of the Adjustment Center's rear exit. Shortly after 3:00 P.M. the main door swung open and Jackson came running out, pistol in hand, with another inmate named Spain close behind. The two of them ran past the yard office where five officers were crouched for cover, and headed downhill toward the yard.

From the balcony gun rail Officer Frank Bortfelt, who had been alerted by the yard officer, shouted out an order: "Jackson, halt!" Jackson answered by firing a shot in the air. Bortfelt then fired a round in return, which ricocheted and hit Jackson in the ankle and calf. The now limping inmate continued to run, so Bortfelt fired another round. This time Jackson fell, breathing his last. Inmate Spain, close behind Jackson but unarmed, dove into the brush, but was quickly apprehended without further incident.

In the meantime several officers rushed to the Adjustment Center, where the main door was still ajar. What they found inside shook even the toughest of these men to their very roots. Inside one of the cells lay a pile of bloody human beings. Sergeant Graham, as well as correctional officers DeLeon and Kasner, was dead. Sergeant McCray was scarcely clinging to life, while officers Breckenridge and Rubiaca, who had managed to free themselves and escape to the lobby area, were still alive, though it looked as if they had been bathed in blood.

An inmate named Ronald Kane was found dead in his cell. He had been beaten and his throat slashed. It appears that Kane, whose cell was on the bar the sergeant was forced to open, refused to go along with the attempted escape and murders. As a result he paid the ultimate price, as did two other inmates who opted not to get involved.

Although I had worked in the Adjustment Center for several years and those inmates housed in the center were considered to be some of the most violent in the prison system, I had never witnessed a bloodier scene than the slaughter that took place at the hands of George Jackson and his cohorts. Defense attorneys, since that awful day in August 1971, have used every legal means possible to delay the trials of the remaining four Soledad brothers, who had now come to be known as the "San Quentin Six," since two other inmates had been added to their group as a result of their participation in the heinous escape attempt. During 1974 Judge Giropoli of the United States District Court of San Francisco scheduled hearings for these men, based on alleged inhumane treatment due to their continued detention in San Quentin's Adjustment Center. The case went on for more than a week, employing two court-appointed attorneys, but was finally dismissed.

Mario Obledo, an appointee of then California Governor Jerry Brown, at one time served as an attorney for one of the San Quentin Six. Obledo was very much involved with all of these inmates, even during his political term as Health and Welfare Director of California. The trials of these inmates were separated, and the time involved in prolonging their trials is the longest in our federal court history, as high court judges, who do not necessarily go along with our laws but rather follow their own "personal convictions" (which at times may run contrary to our criminal laws), continued to find ways to postpone bringing these men to justice.

Sadly, though many died in the Adjustment Center slaughter at San Quentin, some leaving young families behind, George Jackson has become somewhat of a folk hero to many misguided followers. In addition, his attorney, Stephen Bingham, and legal advisor, Vanetta Anderson, were never prosecuted for their obvious involvement in Jackson's escape attempt. Immediately upon leaving the prison that fateful day, Bingham also left the country and stayed in hiding for seven years, until the statute of limitations on his probable involvement had lapsed. Angela Davis, tried and acquitted for her part in the first of the two escape attempts, continues to profit financially from the murderous incident.

Assassin...or Tier Missionary?

One of the more rewarding experiences I had in working with well-known or "infamous" inmates was the time I spent with Sirhan Sirhan, the man convicted in 1968 of killing presidential candidate Robert F. Kennedy. I wouldn't term my relationship with Sirhan a complete success by any means, but it certainly had some positive aspects as compared to my experiences with other inmates, particularly George Jackson.

Sirhan Sirhan was born in Jordan in March 1944, and, along with his parents, came to America as a political refugee in January 1957, not long before his thirteenth birthday. They settled in the Southern California area, but Sirhan's father, Bishara, soon returned to Jordan because he was having difficulty maintaining employment in the U. S. As a result Sirhan's mother, Mary, found work in a Pasadena nursery school and managed to hold the household together.

Sirhan attended public school from the time of his arrival in this country, and soon after took on two newspaper routes, one in the morning and one in the evening. He did this for about four years, and had no difficulty in school. He has been described as a responsible young man and a good student. He enjoyed reading and participating in sports at the Pasadena Boys' Club, as well as his studies in languages, history, and geography. Upon graduation from high school, Sirhan attended Pasadena City College for about one year, where he concentrated on language studies.

Then, in the early part of 1962, Sirhan's younger sister and only sibling, Ida, became ill with leukemia. Her death three years later had a serious effect on Sirhan. He could no longer concentrate on his college studies and eventually dropped out. Soon he was working as a gas station attendant, a job that lasted about seven months. He also worked for a short time as an exercise boy at Santa Anita Race Track. After that he found a job on a horse ranch, but that ended with some injuries resulting from a fall from a horse. A string of other employers found Sirhan to be industrious, but he always seemed to have difficulty accepting authority, which he considered foolish and unnecessary. Before long he started to gamble on the horses, losing consistently.

From 1966 until he shot Robert Kennedy in 1968, Sirhan was involved with the occult and Rosicrucianism, which is the study of ancient mystical, philosophical, and religious doctrines, as well as the application of those doctrines to modern life. This interest in the unusual ways of influencing events and material objects came at a period when Sirhan was still struggling to deal with personal loss in his family and may very well have been searching for answers.

It was during this time that a statement from presidential candidate Senator Robert F. Kennedy caught his attention. Although Sirhan knew little about Kennedy or his politics, he was angered by the candidate's apparent support of Israel and the pledge he made that, were he to become President, he would support that nation by immediately sending them sixteen Phantom jets. Sirhan was known to be irritable and easily angered, particularly when it came to Arab-Jewish conflicts. The Arab defeat in the Six-Day War was a particularly sensitive subject to the former Jordanian. Whatever the final instigation, Sirhan's assassination of Robert Kennedy can only be described as premeditated and deliberate, based on motives and demonstrated by the following evidence:

- A notebook, with handwritten entries by Sirhan, told of his intention to kill Senator Robert F. Kennedy on or before June 6, 1968. His notes also reflected dissatisfaction and hostility toward the United States government and its leaders.
- Sirhan purchased a .22 caliber revolver in January 1968 from George Erhardt. On June 4, 1968, Sirhan spent an excessive period of time on a rifle range, practicing rapid-fire shots. That same night he discharged eight shots from the weapon, hitting and killing Senator Kennedy.

On that fatal day of June 4, 1968, after his extended target practice, Sirhan rode by bus past the Ambassador Hotel in Los Angeles, California. As the traffic became congested, he spotted the campaign meeting that was being held for Senator Kennedy, and he got off the bus. He milled around in the crowd for a while, later claiming that he waited only to see what Kennedy was like in person. He then went into the hotel bar and had a few drinks, waiting for Kennedy to show up. When the senator arrived he was escorted through the hotel kitchen to avoid much of the crowd. Sirhan followed him to the kitchen and, when he had a clear view, took out his pistol and began firing. Sirhan's plan, as outlined in his notes, had been to kill Kennedy before he could be elected President of the United States. Tragically, he succeeded.

Judge H. V. Walker, who presided over the trial in which the Jordanian immigrant was convicted of Kennedy's murder, concurred with the evidence submitted against Sirhan, saying, "I felt the verdicts reached by the jury were the proper ones in view of all the evidence and the law." Following Sirhan's conviction and his subsequent housing at San Quentin, he was handled with great caution by prison officials. His need for protection was not related to negative behaviors while on Death Row, but rather to prevent an incident similar to the slaying of President John F. Kennedy's assassin, Lee Harvey Oswald, by Jack Ruby. The need for this close security continued even after Sirhan, along with 105 other condemned men in California, was released from Death Row by the United States Supreme Court in August 1972. At that time Sirhan was transferred from the row to the Adjustment Center, where he continued in protective custody on a "walk-alone" status, meaning he was not permitted to exercise with other inmates in the open air, but only by himself on the tier. Again, this was for his own protection, though he hated the long-term isolation.

My first close contact with Sirhan was in the latter part of 1972, soon after his transfer from Death Row to the Adjustment Center. My position at that time was as counselor for the center, and it involved much of the legal transition from the condemned sentence to an indeterminate sentence, which carried a seven-year minimum eligible parole. For Sirhan, this meant his earliest possible parole date was May 1976.

From the time I first met Sirhan face to face, I found him to be respectful and willing to talk, though not about his crime. That topic was off limits. But after a few more years in the Adjustment Center, the stress of the walk-alone status began taking its toll on Sirhan. He spent much of his time reading, but complained that he never had enough reading material. One day, as I stood outside his cell, I asked him, "Do you have a Bible, Sirhan?"

He shook his head. "I am not interested in the Bible."

I then said I thought it would be good for him to have some constructive reading material, and I couldn't think of anything better than the Bible. That's when he admitted that he had tried reading the Bible a few times but couldn't understand it. Though I knew little about the paraphrased *Living Bible*, I suggested he give it a try. "It won't disappoint you," I assured him, praying I was right. He didn't respond right away, but as I prepared to walk away from his cell he asked, "Mr. Hare, could you get me one of those books? It sounds good."

I was pleased, though I wasn't too sure if there were any copies of that particular Bible within the prison walls. Then, to be perfectly honest, I got so busy with other matters that I forgot my promise to Sirhan, until a week had passed and, at four o'clock on a Friday afternoon, Sirhan asked me, "Mr. Hare, what happened to the book you promised me?"

Immediately I answered, "Sirhan, I will go and get it right now."

I tried the Protestant chapel first, but it was closed. Then I found the Catholic priest, Father Harrison, in his office. "Do you know where I can get a copy of the *Living Bible*?" I asked him. "I promised one to Sirhan."

"I have no idea," he replied. Then he paused and said, "Wait a minute. Let me check my mail." There was a large manila envelope in the mail, addressed to Father Harrison, with no return address. Inside was a brand new *Living Bible*. The priest handed it to me with a smile and said, "Here's Sirhan's Bible, Joe."

Never ceasing to be amazed at God's perfect timing and provision, I delivered the book the following morning. Sirhan was overjoyed. My advice to him was, "Now, Sirhan, you need a good teacher. And our God has not only given us His Word in the Bible, but also the Holy Spirit to help direct us in our reading it with understanding."

Soon after I gave Sirhan his Bible, he asked me for a job. He needed something to do, he explained, something to break the monotonous routine of long, isolated periods in his cell. "Would you be willing to sweep the tier?" I asked him. He immediately agreed, and from that day forward, the tier was never so clean. It became a common sight to see Sirhan pushing the broom with one hand while holding his Bible in the other, reading as he worked. He often stopped in front of the cells and read portions of the Scriptures to other inmates, pointing out a special promise or nugget of wisdom he'd come across. I soon began to refer to him as our "tier missionary."

Still, despite his Bible reading and tier-sweeping job, Sirhan seemed to be deteriorating. I was concerned about the negative effects of his prolonged walk-alone status, and I tried on three different occasions to have him transferred to the new protective custody unit at Soledad. I was turned down each time. It seems the administration in Sacramento was opposed to the move, as was Sirhan's mother, who was concerned for his safety. And it was a valid concern, of course, as there had been ninety-seven inmates killed by other inmates that year at San Quentin. The general feeling was that Sirhan was safer continuing in his protective walk-alone situation.

I then decided to expand Sirhan's duties, finding assignments for him in my office. As he worked with me in that relaxed atmosphere, our relationship grew and I made it a point to spend a little time each day in conversation with this lonely man. In 1972, as Sirhan's Adult Authority appearance neared, his hopes for parole were rising. "Don't get your hopes too high," I cautioned him. "This is only a review." I then reminded him, as I had done several times before, that regardless of the outcome of his Adult Authority appearance, he had to admit his responsibility for the murder if ever he wanted to move on in his life in a positive direction.

My evaluation of Sirhan would have some bearing on the decision of the Adult Authority, and I had to be completely honest in that evaluation. I included the positive points I had seen while working with Sirhan, but I also included what he had finally told me regarding his crime. He never denied the shooting, in spite of the attempts by his defense to prove an additional bullet was fired, but he hoped that evidence would eventually prove that there truly was another bullet—one not fired by his gun—and that the additional bullet was the one that killed Kennedy, rather than the ones from his own gun. The Adult Authority seemed quite willing to accept my evaluation, with a recommendation for a long parole date. The hearing was positive, with parole being set for 1986, giving Sirhan a total of seventeen years for the crime of Murder First and Assault with a Deadly Weapon with Intent to Commit Murder, five counts. Sirhan, however, was disappointed that his parole date was still so far away. But following my counseling with Sirhan and the immediate approval of the California Director of Corrections, Sirhan was finally moved to the Protective Custody Unit at Soledad, where his adjustment was excellent. This unit was relatively new, having been constructed at Soledad for inmates needing special protection but also including programs designed to help them adjust to their relative long-term isolation. It was ideal for Sirhan, who had been extremely bored and depressed over his walk-alone status at San Quentin.

As for Sirhan's parole date of 1986, it has come and gone, in part because Sirhan's prosecutor later became the California Attorney General and subsequently filed an objection to Sirhan's release. The denial was based primarily on rumors from one of Sirhan's former jail cellmates. This man claimed that just after Sirhan's arrest he had said he would kill the entire Kennedy family if he were ever released. Unaware of his threat against the Kennedy family, I was disappointed that Sirhan's parole was denied at that time, as I thought he would be able to make a productive life for himself if he were returned to his homeland of Jordan. But I was also disappointed at Sirhan's most recent Adult Authority hearing in 1997, when Sirhan claimed to have no knowledge of having committed the crime of murdering Senator Robert F. Kennedy. As a result, Sirhan remains in prison to this day, and most likely will spend the rest of his days there.

I don't mean to imply that I think Sirhan Sirhan shouldn't have to pay the price for his crime, and I personally am a supporter of the death penalty in certain cases. But his death sentence was commuted, and with that in mind, I felt justice would best be served by his release from prison and deportation to Jordan. Despite the outcome of Sirhan's life, however, I will always remember the special relationship we shared during his time as "tier missionary," and I hope and pray that his time spent reading the Bible will not have been wasted.

Murder by Proxy

One of the most notorious criminals of all time, Charles Manson, was also housed at San Quentin. Though he didn't physically participate in the Tate-LaBianca murders in 1969 for which his followers, or "family," were convicted, the jury obviously believed he was the mastermind behind the brutal slayings of these seven individuals. Thus, as reflected in his conviction on eight counts of first-degree murder and his subsequent death sentence, he was judged to be as responsible as those who actually committed the heinous crime—a sort of "murder by proxy," if you will.

Charles "Charlie" Manson was received at San Quentin on the death sentence on April 22, 1971. In August of 1972, however, he—along with 105 other Death Row inmates, including Sirhan

Sirhan—had his sentence commuted to life when the California Supreme Court abolished the death penalty in that state. As a result he was retained in a closed security cell at the Adjustment Center, primarily as protection from the other inmates. Evaluation by prison officials soon determined that Charlie would not adjust anywhere other than the closed security situation he was in at San Quentin, and so, partially due to his own request, he has continued to be housed in protective custody at the Adjustment Center ever since.

In contrast to the years I spent getting to know Sirhan, I was never able to get close to Charlie. Manson simply does not permit anyone to become familiar with him. He trusts no one and seems to care about no one, though he likes to talk, so long as someone else is willing to listen. And so I listened when I could, though I gave little credence to much of what he said.

I soon learned that Charles Manson is a man with little regard for personal cleanliness. If it were up to him, he would never take a shower or put on clean clothes. Even before the grooming orders were so greatly relaxed by the California Department of Corrections, he let his dirty, ungroomed whiskers grow as long as possible. At times he seemed to enjoy changing his personality by suddenly cutting off his long hair and beard. One of his favorite pastimes was playing the guitar he had received from one of his followers, Lynnette "Squeaky" Fromme, prior to her own incarceration, though there never seemed to be any recognizable melody or tune when he played.

Manson never admitted to me any part in the Tate-LaBianca murders, and he claimed he never had any need to tell the others to commit the murders because they already knew what they had to do. He also claimed that the courts and news media created the "family," along with the idea that the family members considered him their "god."

Despite all that, he seldom talked to me without a Bible in his hand, even when he was using profanities, which was much of the time, though he never opened or quoted from the Scriptures. It seems he had requested the Bible from Chaplain Harry Howard, who was surprised at Manson's twisted interest in the Bible and Christianity. Charlie once told the chaplain, "Everyone must come to the cross, either voluntarily or they will be dragged there in judgment." Apparently he has chosen to be dragged there in judgment, because when he referred to God or Jesus Christ it was only as "that man up there," or even "that S.O.B." He seemed to believe those terms reflected his familiarity with the Almighty, though it was obvious through the years that he never accepted the Christian faith or made any sort of commitment to serve God.

Still, I attempted to gain Charlie's confidence by listening to his stories, and tried to steer him in the right spiritual direction when I could, though he was never responsive. One day, as I was passing his cell, he said, "You know, Mr. Hare, you think I'm a devil."

I stopped and thought for a moment, and then said, "Maybe so, Charlie. But remember, my God never made you a devil. You did that all by yourself."

On another occasion Manson attempted to explain why some of the family considered him a god. It seems Charlie was asked to heal one of his follower's children because the child had started walking with a limp. Charlie said he thought there must be some reason for his limping, so he took the little boy aside and checked his shoe. Sure enough there was a nail poking through it. Manson removed it, and the boy's limp was corrected almost immediately. Because Charlie never explained to anyone what had happened, respect for him as a healer soon spread throughout the family.

One subject Manson liked to talk about was love. He said that love is formed by doing things for one another. The girls in the family wanted Charlie to love them, he explained, but Manson dismissed this desire by encouraging them to love him instead. He convinced them that they would then experience great joy because they would want nothing more than to love him. Charlie, however, claimed he was not a lover but a counselor, and that was what those young women needed.

Charlie also claimed that he was being persecuted and that the entire court trial was a sham. He never showed any apparent remorse or even regret for the loss of life he had caused, as he felt that the victims "got what was coming to them."

I must admit, after the times I spent with Charles Manson, I came to believe he should never be released from prison and returned to society. Each time I was around him I sensed something evil, which I can't easily describe, and never once did I see even a hint of sorrow, let alone repentance, for what he had done.

On the other hand, I've heard stories of the conversions of some of Manson's former followers, including Bruce Davis, Susan Atkins, and Charles "Tex" Watson. Though I don't personally know these individuals, others who do have seen evidence of dramatically changed lives. It is reported that when one inmate said to Tex Watson, "The Lord is not going to get you out of prison," Watson replied, "Brother, the Lord has already got me out of prison and set me free."

All I can say is amen to that. As I pointed out earlier, prison changes everyone—for better or worse. The lives I've described in this chapter give clear testimony to that truth, as each chose his direction and his destiny.

> *The Lord is not slack concerning His promise, as some count slackness, but is longsuffering toward us, not willing that any should perish but that all should come to repentance (2 Peter 3:9).*

Chapter 6

Death Row

Death Row. The very words sound dark and ominous. By implication, it is a row of cells full of people condemned to death for their crimes. I spent a lot of my career as a corrections officer/counselor on the Row and got to know many of the Row's inhabitants, but I can't say I ever got used to the idea of what the Row represented.

That doesn't mean I don't believe in capital punishment. As I said at the beginning of the book, I had to settle that issue in my heart before I could accept the job at San Quentin, and I came to the conclusion that there are certain crimes that are so heinous that society must require the ultimate price from the perpetrators. However, having said that, I don't believe for a minute that anyone is beyond redemption. God can and does forgive anyone who turns to Him in true repentance and receives His free gift of salvation through Jesus Christ. It was that balance of understanding that enabled me to work all those years on California's infamous Death Row.

Death Row is an area where only assigned personnel are permitted without special clearance. The Row is usually quiet. For a new officer or staff member the Row is a very different experience, and requires a fresh awareness of everything that is said or done. Death Row residents, according to the law, are legally dead and awaiting execution. The primary concern for most of them is in obtaining a "stay" of execution, which is temporary, or maybe even a new trial or a reversal of their sentence due to a technicality.

There is seldom any positive conversation for inmates on the Row. Many of them have spent a decade or more waiting—and hoping. I wanted so much to tell them about

Jesus, but I couldn't unless one of them opened the door. When anyone did, my first question was, "Where do I start, Lord?" Death Row is undoubtedly the greatest mission field in our land, though few will ever have the opportunity to minister there. My wife, Pat, was a big part of my work with those inmates, as her prayers and support upheld me through every day I was there. She shared in my joys, as well as my sorrows, for she has always been willing to bear an inner pain for those she loves.

Through the many trials of those years, God kept every promise—not only those promises found in His Word, the Bible, but also those He made to me personally. During my years in the Security Housing Units I was exposed to some of the bloodiest days imaginable. I have been in the depths of riots and knife fights when the only way of escape was to walk straight into and through the midst of the battle. My God protected me every time. I was never seriously attacked or injured by any of those hard-core criminals.

God also gave me the ability to speak with the inmates, to communicate with them from my heart. The opportunities to witness and testify for my Lord have been powerful, so long as the inmate first opened the door. It is impossible to estimate the blessings of God during that time, but I know that when the most difficult inmates were in need, my Lord came through.

As a Death Row counselor, I was deeply concerned for the inmates housed there. They were, after all, human beings, creations of God, made in His image. And yet they were legally dead. In fact, when one of them was escorted from one place to another, the escorts would clear the way ahead of them, sometimes even calling out, "Dead man walking." When I made my way down the tiers, I often looked into the faces of those condemned men and silently prayed, *Where do they stand with You, God?* I would offer a greeting to each inmate, but if they didn't respond, I moved on.

One day I came upon a black inmate sitting on his bunk, staring out through the bars of his cell. I stopped and asked, "Can I help you?"

He didn't answer right away, but when he did he asked, "How do you feel about the death penalty?" Needless to say, I was somewhat taken aback, but I answered that I was in favor of it.

"Why?" he asked. "What reason can you give to justify it?"

I called upon the Lord for help, and as I spoke I felt the Lord giving me the exact words to speak. "We have laws," I explained, "many of which were set in place by God for His people, His creation. You and I are subject to God's laws first, but also to the laws of society. If we live by God's laws, the Bible says we have no reason to fear man's law, including the death penalty. If we ignore God's laws, then God says we are still subject to the laws of man. In your case, you were convicted of murdering another human being, part of God's creation."

I paused, and then went on. "The wonderful thing is that my Lord made a sacrifice to pay for our sin—ours, not His. God gave His only Son, Jesus, to die as a sin offering. Now you and I, no matter how wicked our sin, can come to God. Because of Jesus' crucifixion and resurrection, we can be forgiven, all by the blood of Jesus. When we repent of our sinfulness and accept Jesus as Lord, we become clean and receive new life—eternal life with our Father in heaven."

Still there was no response. Then, finally, he asked, "Will I get off the Row?"

Again, the Lord gave me the answer. "When Jesus enters our life, we are born again, not of flesh but of the Spirit. The future is important. Where will you go when you leave this world? The Bible says without Jesus we are subject to eternal damnation—hell. With Jesus we go to a heavenly home with the Father. Now, whether you go from the gas chamber or some other place is unimportant. It is where you are going that counts."

No comment, so I asked him, "Would you like to meet my Jesus?"

"Not right now," he answered. "I want to know more about it first."

I then asked if he was hungry for spiritual food. "If you are," I said, "you'd better eat and be filled."

That was the end of our conversation, and I don't know if that inmate came to any inner decision, but I saw nothing so far as an outward change. Later he was brought before me and other staff members for disciplinary action due to an attack on an officer. The inmate later apologized to me for his attitude. This was a big step on his part, particularly because in the past this African-American had based all his actions on racial hatred. The crime that had put him on Death Row was robbery and murder of his former employer, as well as a female victim who was on the premises at the time.

God used this incident to show me how big a job I had on this row of condemned inmates. He helped me understand that His gift of love was not just for someone I considered receptive and even likeable, but for the fellow who seemed truly unlovable and unworthy—for we are all unworthy of God's great gift.

Death Row is one of the security areas in San Quentin where few visitors are permitted, not because the Department of Corrections has anything to hide, but because of the need for intense security to protect the staff and inmates. The entrance to the Row is from the North Block rotunda. The door is opened upon security clearance. As an iron gate opens, the inner iron door swings open into another area.

To the right is a solid iron door that leads directly to the overnight death cell, which is used only twenty-four hours prior to a scheduled execution. The stairway for emergency entrance to the Row has a locked gate. The elevator to the left is four feet by five feet. When the signal buzzer to the Row is sounded, the elevator moves slowly as it sways and creaks on its ascent.

The sergeant, prior to opening the big iron door, uses a small view window glass to identify the individuals reaching the destination. There is also an inner iron gate. The cells extend the length of the unit, with the showers located in the center. Protective custody and management cells are limited to five on each side. The showers are nine feet by ten feet and have been used for our chapel services on the Row, with eight or ten inmates carrying their stools to the shower area to hear the chaplain minister the Word of God from outside the locked bars.

The inmates on Death Row often talked about the gas chamber and speculated about what it would be like. Some said they would take a deep breath to get it over with, while others said they would breathe normally. Their major concern seemed to be finding the easiest way to die, rather than what would happen to them after death.

The officers assigned to the death detail were carefully chosen, a crew of five with individual duties, but they worked as a team. They were all skillful, professional, attentive, and considerate to the inmates. The warden, chaplain, and usually the chief medical officer were also part of each execution. The warden was responsible to see that the execution was carried out according to the laws of the State of California.

The traditional green carpet was the last part of the holding cell area. The carpet extended from the holding cell to the gas chamber. As the condemned man left the holding cell, he walked down the carpet and saw the chamber for the first time. The two officers followed him closely to his rear. The inmate stepped over the door lip of the chamber and was then seated in the left chair. His glance may have flickered over the many witnesses, some very much against the law of capital punishment, others in favor of it.

The two officers would work rapidly as the inmate was strapped into the chair. One officer might stop to adjust the strap and ask, "Is that better?" Or he might say, "Good luck," as he turned to leave the chamber, maybe even giving a pat on the inmate's shoulder. Once the officers were outside the chamber, the door was shut.

The warden, chief medical officer, and the official executioner stood outside the inner window. The Venetian blinds afforded the inmate some privacy, preventing witnesses from looking directly into his face. The warden gave the signal, and the executioner pulled the lever. The cyanide pellets dropped. The plop could be heard by the inmate. The build-up of the gas took approximately ten seconds, but the inmate's first breath would knock him out. Medical authorities insisted there was an almost instantaneous loss of consciousness. The warden and all the prison personnel were justifiably concerned over the possible feelings of this condemned human being.

Can you imagine our God in a moment like that? Here was a man created in God's own image, sentenced to die for taking the life of another human being. Our Jesus loves that man enough to have died for him and paid the price for his sin.

Death is never a pretty thing, and it certainly isn't entertainment. Death hurts. When the execution is done with precision by the government it is exactly that—an execution, rather than a killing. It is the most extreme form of punishment, and it is ugly. I do not believe a witness to an execution can ever forget it. It is a picture of death that becomes etched in the mind forever.

The gas chamber at San Quentin is enclosed in glass. The octagonal shape permitted full vision of witnesses, with the exception of the blinds that prevent direct gazing into the dying man's face. The inmate usually walked to the chamber with little or no assistance.

I remember one inmate who allowed his eyes to search the faces of the witnesses. I wondered at the time what he was looking for. Then he winked and gave a nod. A Jesuit priest had visited with this man on numerous occasions and was among the witnesses. Perhaps the inmate had been touched by God during one of those visits. Now that inmate was walking through the valley of the shadow of death. I could only hope and pray that he had indeed received Jesus as his Lord and Savior and that the Lord was with him in that very moment. As the door was being sealed, the inmate closed his eyes, and his lips moved slightly as if in prayer. The cyanide pellets dropped, but death did not come quickly. It was obvious this man's body was fighting for life, searching for fresh air that was no longer available. When it was over, he slumped forward, his head on his chest.

This young man was named Alexander Robillard, and he had been convicted of killing a police officer. A cub reporter, just months after being hired, witnessed the execution and stated, "Through the final agonizing moments before death, it was hard to realize fully what was taking place. I had the feeling that this man, clean cut and pale, was not really being killed. But yes, it was true. This was the cold, hard reality of capital punishment."

Today cyanide pellets are no longer used at San Quentin. Instead, in the same chamber, inmates are given a lethal injection, which most believe is more humane.

One of the most difficult death penalty cases I can remember was that of Barbara Graham who, along with her two crime partners, was sentenced to death in 1953. Barbara was born in Oakland in 1923 and, like so many who eventually end up in prison, she had a terrible childhood. Her mother was incarcerated when Barbara was only two years old, and she was then raised by neighbors. She received very little education and became promiscuous as a teenager. Soon she, like her mother, was in trouble with the law.

Though Barbara tried to turn her life around by getting married and having a child, she was quickly divorced and back on her own. Her second marriage lasted less than a year. In and out of prison, Barbara's friends soon consisted of those involved in prostitution and gambling. A third marriage also ended abruptly. Finally she married Henry Graham, but quickly became romantically involved with one of her husband's criminal associates, Emmet Perkins.

By this time Barbara had three children, but her criminal bent was strong, and Perkins had a lot of influence on her. He soon convinced Barbara to help him and two other men, Jack Santo and John True, rob an elderly widow named Mrs. Mabel Monahan. Perkins was convinced that Mrs. Monahan kept large sums of money and expensive jewelry in her home. When they arrived at Mrs. Monahan's house and demanded her money and jewelry, she either couldn't or wouldn't hand it over, and Barbara beat her with a gun and then smothered her with a pillow. True, in exchange for immunity from prosecution, agreed to testify against Barbara, Perkins, and Santo. All three were convicted and received the death sentence.

Barbara was moved to special housing in the San Quentin Muller Hospital in November of that year. Two hospital rooms and a part of a dead-end corridor were converted into a suite at the cost of $14,880, a large sum in those days. Barbara also had special security, which was a fulltime female officer. Barbara was eventually shuffled back to the Corona Prison for Women because of the mounting cost.

Barbara's next return to San Quentin was when she received a date of execution for June 1955. She was transferred directly to the overnight holding cell beside the gas chamber. Her two male crime partners, Santo and Perkins, were already housed on the San Quentin Death Row. Neither of these fellows talked much about the crime or pointed fingers at one another, and I don't remember either of them mentioning Barbara's name. Santo and Perkins were executed together, after no stays or delays of execution.

Barbara was executed alone. It was a stressful situation due to the delay obtained from a judge by Barbara's attorney. She was actually entering the gas chamber when the delay came through, and was then returned to the overnight holding cell. After a couple of hours the execution proceeded. I'm sure the attorney acted in what he felt was the best interest of his client, but if the one-year automatic appeal process had been followed properly, this stressful event would have been prevented.

From all I have seen on the Row, I truly believe that every human being who takes the life of another carries a lot of guilt as a result of his actions, and no punishment can equal that sort of pain. One inmate I knew quite well admitted his guilt and declared that he wanted to die rather than spend the rest of his life in prison. His fear was living with the time, yes, but also with the guilt and pain. As this inmate's automatic appeal date drew near, he asked that there be no delays. Fearing the State of California might overturn capital punishment, he petitioned the court to carry out his sentence of death.

This inmate was considered by some who oppose capital punishment to be mentally unstable. He was examined by a court-appointed psychiatrist, and the report described him as "psycho-neurotic, an emotionally unstable person with chronic alcoholism." The report showed an IQ of 127, placing him in a superior intellectual category. Before his death this inmate declared, "I am guilty of murder. I am guilty of killing another human being. I want to die with some dignity."

Laurence Jackson, another Death Row inmate, felt quite differently. He had twenty-nine hours left before his execution, and he had accepted the fact that nothing was going to happen to stop his execution. He had just said goodbye to his family and was on his way back from the visiting room when a sergeant rushed up to him and, in front of his escort officer, announced, "A Federal Court has granted a stay of execution." It wasn't a reprieve that would save his life, but a temporary delay.

Jackson's reaction is difficult to put into words. He was glad to have a stay, relieved and even hopeful for a complete reprieve. But, of course, he couldn't count on that. He had been sent to Death Row in 1962 for strangling a fifty-two-year-old Southern California woman who had answered his ad for employment. He had three previous execution dates prior to that most recent one before the U.S. Supreme Court struck down the death penalty in February 1972. During those ten years of waiting for execution, Jackson learned to live with the threat of death hanging over him by living one day at a time.

"You start out with a lot of hope," he said. "But as time goes by, that fades. You have to keep some hope, though, because if you give it all up, there's no way to go on."

Jackson saw nine men, including some he knew and liked, take that final trip down to the green chamber. "It's a very sad thing, saying goodbye to a friend and knowing he's going to be dead in a few hours and you'll never see him again…. You can't imagine how that affects you."

As a man's execution date drew near, the other inmates didn't talk about it too much. Jackson explained, "They treat you the same as always. Some may volunteer to help you with your case."

Jackson was forty-eight years old when he made those statements, fourteen years after he first arrived at San Quentin. "I was a very selfish person then. I thought first of myself and what I wanted, and I didn't care who I hurt or how I got it, just as long as I got what I wanted." Fourteen years later, however, he felt he was ready for the mainstream of life. "I'm to the point now that society wouldn't have to worry about me." He was opposed to the death penalty, saying, "It serves no purpose whatever."

Over the years I asked all the residents of Death Row if they had ever stopped and thought about the death penalty before they committed their crimes. Not one of them had, although Jackson said he still thought of the woman he killed. "It's very difficult to live with the knowledge that you've taken someone's life, and you can't reverse it. If I could bring back the victim, giving my life, I wouldn't hesitate."

Unfortunately I never heard Laurence Jackson say, "Lord, I have sinned. Forgive me and make me clean." He worked hard on his case to find a means that might be acceptable to the court. The commute was based on the action of the U.S. Supreme Court finding the death penalty unconstitutional in California, although that penalty has since been restored.

One of the most notorious cases to come out of Death Row in San Quentin was that of Caryl Chessman. His execution actually came as a surprise to many, as it had been postponed for twelve years as Chessman's attorneys filed one appeal after another. Chessman had a prior record and had served time at San Quentin even before his consignment to Death Row for the crime of forced rape. Though he had not committed murder, Chessman was convicted under the "Little Lindburg Law" of kidnapping and bodily harm, established after the infamous kidnapping of well-known aviator Charles Lindburg's baby. I personally remember that kidnapping case, even though I was a child at the time. I lived in New Jersey with my family, not far from the Lindburg estate. Bruno Richard Hoffman was convicted of the crime and sentenced to death in the electric chair, though he died proclaiming his innocence.

Caryl Chessman was tried and convicted as the "Red Light Bandit." Lovers' Lane in Los Angeles, California, was the scene of his crime. Chessman had tied a red bandana over his car's spotlight and impersonated a plainclothes police officer, using a false identification and badge. He came upon a young couple parked in Lovers' Lane and ordered the male from the car and out of sight of the young female. Chessman then took the female to an isolated area and brutally raped her. The crime was so hideous and intense that the young woman was still confined to a psychiatric hospital at the time of Chessman's execution twelve years later.

Due to continued attempts by Chessman to contact the courts and the judge, the entire appeal system for death penalty cases has lost its effectiveness. There exists—on the books—an appeal limit of one year for death penalty cases, and that only on the existence of new evidence. Execution of the sentence is supposed to take place at the end of that year. Needless to say, that is no longer the case, regardless of what is on the books.

The first legal paper Chessman wrote was on toilet paper, which was smuggled out of Death Row and mailed to the court. Chessman claimed the paper was mailed by Death Row officers, who were promptly disciplined. However, the publicity and political reaction to Chessman's paper caused a lot of disruption in the system, changing

Death Row procedures and extending the right to court action by all state inmates. Writs and appeals now flow freely. Though some good has come out of these changes, our legal system and the promise for swift justice has been completely lost, particularly with capital punishment.

Caryl Chessman was considered a genius due to his ability to use technicalities and delays of execution, most of which was accomplished by Caryl acting as his own attorney. His abilities and knowledge to do all these things were gained almost exclusively from the Death Row legal library, which was set up by order of the court to assure all condemned inmates access to the courts.

Whereas before it had been necessary to present new evidence in order to file an appeal, it was now necessary only to prove that an inmate did not have full access to the court during his trial. This was the concern of the High Court. Caryl Chessman was finally executed despite his legal attempts, but not before leaving a legacy of technical and legal maneuvering that would impact the courts and penal system for years to come. Chessman, through his evasive tactics, inspired thousands of inmates to attempt to "beat the rap" through a technicality.

I personally believe this change undermines the hope for rehabilitation. Legal maneuvering may bring about the commute of a sentence, but it does nothing to encourage an inmate to face himself and his crimes and then turn to God for forgiveness. When the Reverend Billy Graham came to San Quentin in 1958, the Master's hand touched many inmates with repentance and salvation, including inmates on Death Row. Though their temporal sentences weren't commuted, they had the promise of eternal life.

In May 1976 the *Independent Journal* of San Rafael in Marin County, California, requested a visit and possible tour of Death Row at San Quentin. In considering the request, the warden and his staff were most concerned for the feelings of the forty-nine male residents on the Row at that time. After much conversation and discussion with these inmates, it was decided to permit one reporter to interview all the residents who agreed to the visit.

These inmates ranged in age from twenty-nine to fifty-six. Harry Harding was the senior resident, and Harold Hill the junior. When Harold was twenty-three he was driving a stolen car when a Highway Patrol officer stopped him for a defective headlight. Hill shot and killed the officer. Eugene Allen, another young inmate, was also sentenced to death at the age of twenty-three after fatally stabbing an officer at the Deuel Vocational Institute. Allen was being held at Deuel on an Amador County conviction for killing another inmate during an escape attempt in another facility. One other inmate participated in the stabbing. At twenty-five, Ernest Graham was convicted of stabbing to death an officer at Deuel Vocational Institute. Thirty-three-year-old John Lawrence Miller killed his mother and father shortly after being released from prison where he had served time for the murder of a two-year-old child. Miller shot his mother in the back of the head, then shot his father five times. John's brother Steven Miller, when he was twenty-three, was convicted of two counts of murder. Along with John and another man, Steven had gone to a motel for a robbery. The victim grabbed for Steven's gun and shot the robber who had accompanied the Miller brothers. Steven Miller was also convicted of killing a police officer in a shoot-out preceding his capture.

These are just a few of the forty-nine men who resided on Death Row at that time. They were all given the opportunity to talk with the reporter, whose name was Pat Angle. Pat then wrote a lengthy article and placed it on the front page of her newspaper. Here are some of the excerpts:

> *They have killed and now they, themselves, are living in the shadow of death. The shadow is not so menacing as it was 15 years ago, when inmates regularly said goodbye to their fellow prisoners and left to die in the green gas chamber five stories below.*

> *In those days, the tension and foreboding on the Row were almost palpable as an execution day approached at San Quentin.*

> *No one seems to expect that swift approach to his execution day. Life on The Row proceeds in a relatively smooth and unchanging routine. It is almost possible for a visitor to forget that the average-looking men there, going quietly about their daily activities, have been condemned to death at some future date and time, yet to be appointed.*

> *The people of The Row are very much aware that their lives are in a balance. Even at this time, judges, after many years, take very surprising actions.*

The article covered three full pages, with mug shots of each of the men on Death Row.

Not too many years ago, the United States Supreme Court deliberated the fate of capital punishment throughout the United States. In 1973 the California State Supreme Court ruled the death penalty unconstitutional, and the United States Supreme Court followed suit. A few months later the Federal Court said the punishment was applied illegally because it gave judges and juries the discretion of imposing either death or life in prison. The Court indicated death would be constitutional if it was made mandatory for certain crimes.

Following the High Court ruling, the 106 people then waiting to die at San Quentin, including mass-murderer Charles Manson and Robert Kennedy's assassin, Sirhan Sirhan, had their sentences commuted.

For more than one year after that there was no longer a Death Row at San Quentin. Its denizens were transferred to other state prisons or shifted into the San Quentin general population. Then, in November 1972, California voted by a two-to-one margin to bring back the death penalty. In September 1973 the State Legislature restored capital punishment for certain criminals: hired assassins; police slayers; life-term inmates who kill guards; mass and repeat murderers; train wreckers; those who kill witnesses to crimes; those who commit murder during a rape, robbery, kidnapping, burglary, or lewd acts involving children.

Although the Row was officially reinstated in January 1974, executions have taken place at a very slow pace since that date. There are currently more than fifty challenges to capital punishment that have gone as far as the United States Supreme Court. The Court's actions continue to uphold capital punishment, and Death Rows are again filled to capacity. The uncertainty is unimaginably intense for those awaiting their executions. The uncertainty is not limited to the condemned, but extended to their families, who undoubtedly experience immense pain and suffering as a result.

One condemned inmate once told me, "The hardest part isn't dying; it's the waiting and wondering, and just not knowing what's going to happen."

People on Death Row have received the death sentence for their crimes against humanity. These people include college graduates, long-time losers, high-school dropouts, alcohol abusers, drug abusers, lifetime criminals, farmers, postal clerks, electricians, butchers, mechanics, accountants, general contractors, small businessmen, and street bums—those who are chronically unemployed.

Their personalities vary as surely as their professions. People who do not know these fellows expect them all to be monsters, but they are not. For those who are willing to look deeply enough, most can find an appealing side to their nature. In many ways they are just ordinary people like you and me. But the residents of Death Row, whatever their qualities, are living under extraordinary circumstances.

For instance, a typical day for a Death Row resident begins at 7:30 when breakfast is served in the individual cells. Death Row inmates are better able to get exercise than they were years ago, as there is now an open yard on top of the unit, so most of their exercise is outside in the fresh air. I often saw inmates sunbathing, reading, talking, playing basketball, and jogging. The high wire fence surrounding the yard makes it impossible for the inmates to see anything on or about the prison grounds.

Death Row inmates shower daily, and Sunday church services or Bible readings are attended by a limited number. Dinner is served at 3:30 in the afternoon, and then the Row is locked down for the night, although residents can type, read, watch TV, or play instruments until one in the morning.

Educators and art teachers come on the Row at least once a week, offering varied opportunities for the men. A visit or even an interview with a staff member can break the monotonous routine of a life set by the reality of capital punishment. The varied ways in which residents of Death Row react to this restricted way of existence are a reflection of their individual personalities.

One cell might contain almost no personal items. An unmade bed may be the only sign that a human being actually lives there. By contrast, another cell resembles a minute but cozy studio, with a bookcase and table carefully fashioned from cardboard, a wall full of pictures (often colorful scenes or naked women), homemade shelf paper on the cell's single shelf, and a neatly made bed with slippers tucked underneath.

For many of the Row inmates, adjusting to the restricted way of life can take months to accomplish. Some never make the adjustment, becoming withdrawn and spending most of their time sleeping. Others do anything they can to get any kind of drugs to ease their pain. There are also those inmates who spend their every waking moment working on their cases, looking for a loophole that might miraculously reverse their sentence of death.

Lawrence Hill, a former operating engineer, had never been in prison before coming to Death Row. A grandfather, Hill claimed he had no complaints about his life. "I am treated very well. The people here are nice to me," he said as he dusted the bars and the shelf in his cell. Reading legal material and writing letters were his main activities.

Edward Conover dealt with his incarceration and death sentence by imagining himself as still running the muffler shop in the Pleasant Hill area of California. Another man in his early twenties studied theology. He also learned to play the guitar, something he had always wanted to do. "I spend a lot of time writing to different church pastors, telling them how I feel about life and a God I never knew," he said. He received a lot of response to his letters and made many new friends, asserting, "My beliefs are what keep me going."

The first condemned man to be received on the Row in May 1974 under the new enactment of capital punishment was a thirty-seven-year-old Caucasian named David. Along with a forty-four-year-old man named John, David had committed the double murder of a sixteen-year-old girl and her nineteen-year-old boyfriend. The two men, in a violent robbery, beat the young couple to death with a tire iron. David was later converted and baptized at the prison chapel. The instability in this man's life, including slitting his wrists in a suicide attempt, was the cause, at his request, of being placed in Protective Custody.

Another young twenty-two-year-old Caucasian was convicted of kidnapping a thirty-three-year-old housewife, raping her, and then murdering her by feeding her strychnine. This individual did not seem to outwardly accept or even recognize his crime as punishable. He had little or no communication with the staff or other inmates.

Angelo, a twenty-eight-year-old African-American inmate, was convicted of murder, arson, sex perversion, robbery, and then the rape of the victim's wife, after which he set fire to the couple's apartment. Angelo worked for a short period as a postal clerk. He could be pleasant, although his racial feelings were often used to justify his actions. Angelo never admitted his guilt; however, the evidence against him was by no means circumstantial. He never openly rejected God, but I was not aware that he ever accepted Him, either.

Julian was a thirty-year-old Mexican-American, a little guy about five feet tall and weighing ninety-nine pounds. He was a mousy type, but was considered very dangerous. His homosexual involvements were excessive, both in and out of prison. Protection for Julian was a twenty-four-hour problem because of gang involvement from the Mexican Mafia, the New Familia, and the Aryan Brothers. Julian used different individuals from these various tips, and actual war broke out between them due to his homosexual behavior.

Shortly after his release from the San Quentin Adjustment Center and parole to the Sacramento area, Julian was charged and convicted of the murders of two elderly Sacramento women. However, his needs were still taken care of with very liberal financial assistance from homosexuals within our society. Julian received gifts of electric typewriters, color televisions, fancy shirts, and silk underwear, though there appeared to be no gratitude from this young fellow. He struck me as a complete Judas, and he proved to be extremely aggressive toward the prison's custodial staff.

Julian spoke with a whine in his voice, and he did not seem to know how to accept any type of refusal. His long-term incarceration in the Protective Custody Unit prior to his parole was upon his own request. Each time I spoke with Julian at his cell, he kept his voice at a low whisper or requested to be taken to my office where we could speak more freely. His complaints usually started with information— who was going to kill someone else on the tier, etc. Then Julian would make his pitch, usually for some special consideration, which was not permissible. I repeatedly found him to be a liar and a cheat.

The Parole Department delayed Julian's parole because there was no conceivable reason to believe this young man would ever make a parole adjustment. Finally the release was made to Sacramento, where he was to be assisted by a homosexual group. Julian made many enemies during his time on the streets between Sacramento and San Francisco, and he never obtained any sort of employment.

The two elderly women he eventually killed—an eighty-year-old deaf mute and a sixty-four-year-old—were sexually molested and their clothing pulled up over their heads and upper bodies, which enabled Julian to smother and strangle the older victim, who finally died from heart failure. The second victim was strangled with a lamp cord after her body had been exposed and molested.

Julian also admitted the killing of a seventy-seven-year-old male during a burglary in 1970. There were no further trials due to the death sentence on the current murders, which had taken place within a week of each other.

Once on Death Row, Julian was kept in a special area on the tier where other inmates were not permitted. Again, this was because of his own request for Protective Custody. Julian showed no interest or desire to seek Jesus Christ; he wanted only his own way of life and had no remorse for his sins or crimes.

Ray was a young Mexican, twenty years old, who had been convicted in the Sacramento murder of a five-year-old girl whom he had enticed into a vacant apartment, then sexually molested, beat, and stabbed to death with a broken bottle. Her tiny, mutilated body was found in a closet a few days later. Ray continued to deny he killed the child, although the evidence was not circumstantial but factual. He also had a past history of sex perversions.

Ray claimed to have turned to the Lord. He was a Roman Catholic and requested approval for marriage to a young woman who mothered his child and also had two other children by other men. Ray never made any outward confession of his crime, continuing to deny or rationalize it. There seemed to be little if any attempt to find the reason for this hideous murder of a child, though he expressed deep love for the young woman he eventually married, as well as for her children.

My continuous delays in recommending approval for this marriage request were related to the hang-ups of sex offenses of the female children. Ray found those reasons unacceptable and even unconstitutional, according to the new director's rules for permissible marriages.

Another inmate, a black thirty-year-old named Billy Joe, had served time in other prisons in the United States, as well as in California. He was convicted in Los Angeles on two counts of murder for kidnapping. Billy Joe raped the young Caucasian woman, then strangled her and beat her to death with a rock. The woman's child was also beaten to death by this big, rough-looking fellow who had fought as a professional heavyweight boxer. There seemed little need for the use of a weapon in this crime. Billy Joe was obsessed with racial hatred for the whites. There was no apparent discretion of individualism with Billy Joe, and he never admitted his actions, though he rationalized and condoned them because of his racial feelings.

Billy Joe proved to be a real problem among staff and inmates. He was a very insecure person who refused to talk about himself or his criminal history. He considered his convictions to be based on racial discrimination and persecution. There was never any evidence that might indicate Billy Joe had a change of heart, even though I attempted to help him on numerous occasions.

Another case that was hard to understand was that of a fifty-six-year-old businessman named Harry, who was convicted of hiring two men to kill his estranged wife by shooting her from a passing car. All three of these partners in crime were on the Row.

Harry offered one of these two men, a thirty-seven-year-old muffler shop owner, a price for the murder. This man then contacted a thirty-two-year-old man to do the job for a fraction of the price Harry had offered. Harry, of course, claimed to have had no part in any of this murder-for-hire transaction.

Harry had been the owner of the farmers' market in a California city. He was also a former major in the U.S. Army. He had reared his family and operated a prosperous business. His wife was part of the enterprise and was possibly influenced by feelings of independence. Her eventual involvement in another business venture led her into a partnership with a man who apparently became more than a business partner. This caused marital problems that led to talk of a divorce. Harry rejected his wife's demands, which evidently led to her threat to expose him to the Internal Revenue Service for tax fraud related to their business. This threat became Harry's motive for murder.

As an employee of the prison system of California, I found myself very cautious about being taken in by an inmate's story of innocence. With Harry, however, I had a hard time putting the evidence together with his personality. The pieces just did not seem to fit, yet the evidence against him was astounding.

I had many opportunities to talk with Harry, and he was receptive to the Spirit of the living God, though he never made any outward commitment to the Lord.

Between late 1955 and 1965 there was a spiritual revival going on among the Death Row inmates. According to one of the correctional officers who worked on the Row at that time, "The Row shower, where church services were conducted, got a little crowded." Individual inmates requested the chaplain to baptize them, and a weekly Bible study was a popular part of this very unusual life on Death Row.

Understandably, many of the Row's residents had great concerns about dying. I got to know many of those fellows over the years, and developed a personal liking for some. I always try to look for the good in everyone, since I believe all of us are made in God's image and therefore have some good in us, regardless of what we have done. As a result I have discovered kindness and compassion in some of the most hardened criminals. I have also found that the very fact of being condemned to death makes people think about things they would never consider otherwise.

Most of the men on Death Row knew they could talk to me, even about their personal problems. I encouraged them to do that, because another belief of mine is that running water can make us clean. When people begin to explore and talk about the things buried deep within, the water begins to flow and anything can happen. Anytime I heard of an inmate getting a disciplinary report, I would go to him and ask if he wanted to talk about it. I guess that's one of the reasons I got the nickname "Papa Joe" during my many years of working with these men.

Many Christians, including myself, accept and even condone capital punishment. I realize there are others who don't, even though we base our beliefs on the same Bible. I have searched God's Word, both as a Christian with a responsibility to obey God and as a former employee of the California Department of Corrections with a responsibility to obey my government. Following are some of the Scriptures upon which I base my beliefs regarding this very important issue:

> *"Surely for your lifeblood I will demand a reckoning; from the hand of every beast I will require it, and from the hand of man. From the hand of every man's brother I will require the life of man. Whoever sheds man's blood, by man his blood shall be shed; for in the image of God He made men" (Genesis 9:5,6, NKJV).*

> *"Now these are the judgments which you shall set before them: ...He who strikes a man so that he dies shall surely be put to death. However, if he did not lie in wait, but God delivered him into his hand, then I will appoint for you a place where he may flee. But if a man acts with premeditation against his neighbor, to kill him by treachery, you shall take him from My altar, that he may die. And he who strikes his father or his mother shall surely be put to death" (Exodus 21: 1,12-15, NKJV).*

Let every soul be subject to the governing authorities.
For there is no authority except from God, and the
authorities that exist are appointed by God. Therefore
whoever resists the authority resists the ordinance of God,
and those who resist will bring judgment on themselves.
For rulers are not a terror to good works, but to evil.
Do you want to be unafraid of the authority? Do what
is good, and you will have praise from the same. For he
is God's minister to you for good. But if you do evil, be
afraid; for he does not bear the sword in vain; for he is
God's minister, an avenger to execute wrath on him who
practices evil (Romans 13:1-4, NKJV).

These scriptures are meant to be a guide and taken with great understanding. I do believe obedience to the earthly authority is a general rule. Sometimes we can see injustice and even want to disobey the rule, but we must realize this is the law. (The only exception would be if the law of man directly violated the Law of God.)

The consequences of violating the law, whether man's or God's, can be severe. The Bible talks about the right to "bear the sword." Only the government has that right, with a responsibility to protect society. Laws are made by those in authority, and people must respect and abide by those laws.

My conclusions about capital punishment have come about after many years of maturity and experience in my profession. Through prayer, as well as searching and pondering God's Word, I have come to an understanding that has brought truth and peace to my heart. I cannot relate the commandment "Thou shalt not kill" to the laws of capital punishment. The same words of that commandment relate to a criminal murder, as the footnotes of the King James Revised Standard Version explain. The commandment does not include the judicial taking of a life or killing in war. Sometimes God's wrath is carried out through civil government when it punishes a wrongdoer.

I personally have never had a problem accepting capital punishment. However, better understanding and compassion have made me realize there is much to be done in the ministry of Jesus Christ to each and every resident of Death Row, for their time is truly short.

I once had the 4:00 P.M. until midnight duty with a condemned man. We talked about his last meal and his fear of death. "Where do I go from here?" he asked me. I took that as my opening and so I started with a question as to whether or not he believed in a "higher power," and our discussion developed from there. Without a clear answer to the question of where we go after death, an inmate can easily become engulfed in fear.

Seeking God for direction is what gave me the peace and wisdom to answer questions like these, for it is only as I walk with God that I am able to truly walk with others.

> *Because the foolishness of God is wiser*
> *than men, and the weakness of God*
> *is stronger than men (1 Corinthians*
> *1:25, NKJV).*

Chapter 7

"The Impact of Societal Changes"

In 1949, not long after I had begun working at San Quentin, Governor Earl Warren sought to make changes in the prison system, seeking to strengthen rehabilitation rather than focus solely on punishment. Convicts were to be called inmates; guards became officers; inmates would be known by their names rather than numbers; prison garb would become less stringent. They were simple changes, meant to instill mutual respect between corrections officers and inmates; for the most part the changes were positive. Before getting into specifics, however, I'd like to discuss a little about my own philosophy of dealing with inmates and how I came to develop and practice those philosophies.

The Bible verse that says "When I was in prison you visited me" had little significance to me until I started working at San Quentin. Over the years I have found myself responsible not only to the California Department of Corrections, but also to my God and His creation, which in my case meant the inmates of one of the largest and most notorious penal institutions in the world. During that time I have learned that my God meant exactly what He said in the Scriptures: Pray without ceasing. I have also realized that not everyone can work in a prison setting. Of course, as I've mentioned before, that wasn't the job I had planned for myself, but apparently God did. I now consider it a privilege, as well as a special and unique calling, and I am very proud of having been a part of it, for nearly every decision I made was relative to the well-being of a human being created in God's image.

My experience over the years in my church has been very rewarding, as it prepared me to do the work of evangelism. Along with others from the church I had the opportunity to go into homes and speak with people about the good news of God's salvation, though not all were receptive. One of the primary things I learned from those visitations with my church was that God places His servants exactly where He wants them. It was a lesson I applied daily in my work at San Quentin.

Personal counseling quickly became part of my daily responsibilities. I must admit there were times I was spellbound by the boldness of the Holy Spirit as He used me in proclaiming Jesus Christ to the inmates in my care. I also learned that we must first receive blessings from God if we are to give blessing to others. I therefore made it my daily priority to talk with Jesus before talking with others.

Throughout my years as a corrections officer my day began at six o'clock. Pat and I would have breakfast and spend time with our Lord, praying and meditating and reading the Scriptures. This set the tone for our day, the focus of all we would do or say, which was: **Jesus is Lord**. We knew that when we were anointed by our Lord we were able, by grace, to do all things with power. On occasion Pat and I got up late and shortchanged the Lord, as well as ourselves, which limited my morning conversation with Jesus to my fifty-minute commute. But my God is understanding and His love is unconditional, even though the day seemed to lack that special something that comes only from spending time in His presence.

I believe God places His servants in situations where we ourselves cannot possibly compete, simply so we will learn to depend on Him. My job at San Quentin certainly did that for me. I quickly discovered that prison was not populated with men who were there for singing too loudly in church. In fact, their language consisted primarily of a peculiar prison jargon, peppered with profanity. I have to admit, however, that in my early years without Jesus my own language included profanity. In fact, there were times I outdid some of the inmates in that area.

In my home life as a boy, my mother was the one who always told us of God's love and made sure we said our prayers at night. My father was never a church-goer, nor did he ever speak of God's love. But he was somewhat of an example to us, in that he taught us the importance of honesty and hard work, even during the Great Depression. (Thankfully, when he was in his nineties, he finally came to the point of accepting Jesus Christ as his Lord and Savior.)

Our God meets His creation, His people, individually, right where they are, and He knew exactly what I needed to bring me to a point of spiritual commitment and maturity in my life. My wife once shared with me about something that happened with our then seven-year-old daughter, Carol. She wanted to go to a movie matinee with her cousin one Sunday. When Pat told her no, Carol responded, "What's the difference, Saturday or Sunday?" This incident caused Pat and me to ask God to guide us in search of a steady church home, as we had not been attending regularly at that point. Maturity in the Lord takes study and prayer, but God had given me a wonderful Christian wife, and He was leading us step by step.

During those early years as a born-again Christian, part of the breaking in me was related to my foul tongue. Can you imagine how I could ever tell an inmate of Jesus when my tongue was so filthy? It was impossible, so I found myself under heavy conviction. At lunchtime I would go into the office in the cellblock to eat, lowering the shade as I studied the Scriptures.

I had developed another hang-up as well. During my early days at San Quentin the inmate's number was more important than his name, and convict was a commonly used term for the men incarcerated there. The Lord had a big job to do in me, for He wanted me to recognize these men as individuals and part of His creation. The question of how to do that was of little significance to me at the time, though I soon learned that I needed to show respect to the inmates and call them by name.

Then seemingly overnight prison reform was on the move. Support and therapy groups were started at San Quentin. Group size quickly expanded from twelve to forty-five, and one even grew to sixty-five. The non-professional staff was finding a complete new way of relating to men they had previously considered convicts with no personal identification.

My counseling group that met at six in the evening grew into a second group that met two hours later, at eight. I had learned to pray before each meeting, asking God for a special anointing to lead the group, and to use me as a means of leading those men to Him. The Lord knew that many of those inmates were not interested in knowing Jesus and that my knowledge of the Scriptures was limited, but I prayed, and God answered.

Soon the Yokefellow Prison Ministry was introduced at San Quentin by a young man named Larry Baulch, an inmate I had met years earlier when he was a three-time loser serving time in San Quentin. Larry had since accepted Christ with the help of former San Quentin chaplain Byron Eshelman. Larry, assisted in the Yokefellow ministry by some fine Christian people, had been given this wonderful opportunity by the founder of Yokefellow Prison Ministries, Reverend Cecil Osborne. Reverend Osborne enabled Larry to attend the San Francisco Baptist Seminary, where he was ordained and committed his life to service in this excellent ministry. I praise the Lord each time I think of Larry, for he was just one more individual God used in His long process of molding me into what He had purposed for my life.

Yokefellow appealed to the prison system under the new reform, and I believe my God used it in helping me in my own learning, as I studied so I could help others. The many hours were all voluntary, and the inmates seemed to sense the difference when the staff was willing to put in extra hours without pay. The approach was based on a form of Christian therapy, meaning they counseled and worked with these men from a biblical viewpoint. The specific direction of each group was determined by the group leader.

God has His ways of bestowing rewards. There was a young man who seemed to be disliked by many of the other inmates. I believe his attitude toward the world was greatly responsible for his very obese condition. The only name he responded to was TD. This young fellow was the son of a top law official in one of our larger California cities. The father had apparently rejected TD after he committed the tragic crime of murder. Eventually the father was eased out of his official capacity and became a police chief in a smaller town.

TD came to our meeting with a complaint that someone was trying to get even with him by putting his name on the Yokefellow list. TD soon became a regular attendee of the group, though he had little to say, and his attitude caused others to dislike him.

One evening I requested that we tape our meeting, and the following week we would play the tape. The response was good, and I had truly called on the Lord to show each one of us what we are like and how we sound to others. I truly felt the presence of the Holy Spirit as the men relaxed and didn't focus on the fact that they were being recorded. There were a few testimonies and some scripture reading, and then TD asked if he could say something. I granted permission, but when he hesitated, I asked, "TD, would you like to close with a word of prayer?"

After a few hushed moments, he began. "Oh, Lord, I don't know how to pray. I don't know what to say." Then the most beautiful words of repentance poured forth: "I don't want to kill ever again. I don't want to hurt anyone. Please forgive me for what I have done. I'm sorry, Lord."

The meeting was silent, as others sensed a difference with TD, who had by that time served approximately twenty years. He later began using his full name, and his father came to accept him once again.

TD came a long way. His mother was hurt by the criminal behavior of her son, but she was not ready to give up on him. Our first telephone conversation seemed to be the answer to her prayers, which basically consisted of, "Some day, Lord, You will touch my son and he will answer You." Over the years I have lost all contact with TD who was serving a life sentence for murder, but God knows exactly where he is today.

The Yokefellow Prison Ministry has helped men to see and accept Jesus before they realized what was happening. As a counselor I found that psychotherapy can help only the individual who is receptive. That individual must want to face facts and to admit what he has done wrong. Reality Therapy has been my source for many years. There is no place to put the blame: each one must face the reality of what he did to be put in prison, and then admit that it was wrong. Then we can begin to explore why he did it, and what we can do to assure he won't do it again. Those changes must then be implemented if there is to be any success.

I don't personally believe in people trying to pull themselves up by the bootstraps. In fact, I believe that's why so many fail. We all need help, and God stands ready to give it when we humble ourselves and ask. So many times during those years I prayed for my God's direction and assistance, and then the doors opened and I found myself with the opportunity to counsel one of the inmates. Again, I would pray, and God gave me the words of wisdom that I needed.

The California Department of Corrections is full of felons, most of whom committed crimes related to a personal weakness. One whose weakness is alcohol started out with just one drink, the addict with just one hit or fix. The gambler, the check forger—they all started small, but their problems grew as they succumbed to their individual weakness. Those weaknesses eventually led to grave habits, and finally became the primary source or motivation for their acts of serious crime.

My experience with these related problems has strengthened my faith, for I know of no power or medication that might help these people like calling upon the name of the Lord. I know my God has heard the cry of the repentant and the oppressed, for He is ready and willing to meet us right where we are—and usually that's at the bottom because few of us acknowledge the need for God until we have tried everything else and nothing is left.

My very good friend Jack Bowen was a tremendous help in starting my career. He was a school psychologist and was always interested in my work with the prison system. Jack introduced me to the book *Reality Therapy* by Dr. William Glasser. He believed my approach to working with the inmates was so close to Glasser's that he first thought I was a student of that teaching. I do have much respect for the writings of Glasser, and I do point out that my profession is that of a counselor who is deeply concerned and experienced with human behavior. My counseling, however, is centered in the Word of God, with the guidance of God's Holy Spirit. As a counselor I had many opportunities to have serious talks with the inmates. Again, the need for the Holy Spirit's guidance was crucial. Many times I was amazed at the boldness with which God used His words through me. As a counselor rather than a chaplain, I always had to allow the inmate to introduce God into a conversation. Then, once the door was open, I had to have something real and dynamic to offer, which is why I knew I needed to spend time with my God every day.

As a family man, my wife and two daughters have been among my greatest blessings. The relationship and many joys we've shared together have prepared me in counseling from a realistic point of view. My wife and I have truly become one in the Spirit. We work well together when teaching, as we did when rearing our children. A teacher must study and prepare before teaching others. God's Word is the food I used for my own studies and to serve to others, and that food must be served in a tasty manner and with special tact and preparation.

I recall sharing with my group a film Pat and I had directed at our church. The Junior High fellowship was well attended, with approximately fifty-five young people each Sunday evening. It was during the winter, and the interest in making the film was keen. The life of Peter was the chosen subject. Each student was given the opportunity to take part. The script was prepared, and then during the spring and summer, we did the casting for the film, which was titled *Upon This Rock*. Numerous church people have since viewed this amateur film production.

About fifty inmates in my group wanted to see the film. The Holy Spirit definitely put His professional touch upon it, and the young people who were part of the production found a more personal meaning and knowledge of the Apostle Peter. The Scriptures were a source of learning and feasting, as the inmates were exposed to the realities of Peter's life and the Christian witness of all the young people involved, as well as mine and my family's. It was a wonderful opportunity to share God's love with these men.

My family has always been considerate and loving toward former inmates who contact me. One Sunday morning a church usher informed me that a young couple would like to speak with me. I wondered who they might be, and as I was walking over to meet them, the Lord revealed to me that the man's name was Edward. He had come through the Guidance Center at San Quentin about six years earlier. I recalled my many conversations with Edward when we discussed Jesus, though at the time I was a very new convert myself and knew little about the Lord. However, God used my limited knowledge and sealed my words to Edward's memory, for he had even remembered the name of my church and had come to see me.

The young woman was Edward's new bride. He was so proud of her and wanted her to meet someone he felt had played a critical part in changing his life for the better. My family and I brought Edward and his wife home for pie and coffee. Oh, how great is our God! He truly can perform miracles, for little did I know years earlier when I talked with Edward that God would use my simple testimony to help change an inmate's life.

After Edward and his wife left for home, Pat reminded me of the time way back in 1949 when Warden Clinton Duffy conducted one of the first tours for prison employees and their wives. It was on a Saturday evening. Two hundred of us gathered outside the prison walls. Warden Duffy led the tour, starting at the gas chamber, then going past the overnight death cells where the condemned men spend their last hours.

The night was dark. It had rained during the day, and the skies were cloudy. Those of us on the tour followed behind an old-timer who carried a lantern. His name was George, and he had been convicted on thirty-five counts of murder. George was considered very dependable by nearly everyone at San Quentin. That night bears many memories, and also marks progressive changes.

The walls of San Quentin were gray cement, unpainted, as were the cells. The lighting was mostly located outside the doorways, making a flashlight a normal piece of the night officer's equipment. The cells were all double, meaning there were two men per cell, except for maximum security and Death Row inmates. The bunkbeds had no sheets or pillowcases, and the only light was a low-wattage bulb hanging from the ceiling. Radio was limited to earphones connected to the two prison radio stations. All lights went out at ten, and the prison became very quiet.

Those of us on the evening tour were later entertained by some of the most talented of the inmate population. The show was followed by a steak dinner in the mess hall, served by a select group of inmates. The tour was a tremendous success, as the inmates involved enjoyed the evening right along with the prison staff and their families.

But much has changed since 1949, the year when prison reform really began to take off. The Correctional Industries became part of the California Department of Corrections, producing a wide variety of goods. My position at the time it was established was in the furniture factory. I was a vocational instructor where all special design office furniture was made. Some of the most exclusively designed buildings in California are furnished from San Quentin.

The Marin Civic Center was one of the finer building projects in Marin County. The San Quentin furniture factory was given the opportunity of making all the special design furniture for the project under the direction, drawings, and plans of the very renowned architect of the development, Frank Lloyd Wright. I am very proud of all the work done in the San Quentin furniture factory. At the time I supervised an average of fifty men who worked for me in an apprenticeship training program, approved and accepted by our trade union. When these fellows were released, they were equipped to obtain suitable employment.

Correctional Industries wanted something different, so invitations were sent to many who might be considered as potential employers for the inmates, asking them and their wives to come and tour the prison and see what the inmates did in these programs. The areas normally considered closed were cleaned and opened for the occasion, even a spot known as "the alley," which has long been considered the most dangerous area of San Quentin.

My then teenaged daughter, Sharon, my wife, Pat, and other friends were among the invited guests for this special tour. Pat and Sharon became so interested in the work on display in one of the shops that they were left behind by the tour. Though they soon caught up with the others and everything turned out fine, our daughter remembers that experience to this day.

Every type of shop was set up and manned by selected inmates who pledged themselves to make that evening a success. The areas were policed by inmates, while the correctional officers with walkie-talkies were used as overseers. The vocational bake shop put out pastries that could have shamed the best of society's bakeries. I'm sure many of the inmates who were a part of that evening wondered what would come of it all.

Those men, like the inmates today, were all human beings who needed to be given a certain amount of trust so they might feel that society is truly a healthy environment, one in which they could be a functional part. I recall introducing my wife and friends to a few of my choice inmates, and I believe that night altered the entire environment of the prison.

The changes within the prison system since I first started working at San Quentin are many. The entire institution has been painted and now maintains a full-time employee who supervises and trains inmates in the vocation of painting. The cells can be painted in a variety of colors to suit the inmates' tastes. Sheets, pillowcases, fluorescent wall fixtures, cell radios, portable televisions, hot and cold water are all part of the improvements. The lighting in and around the institution is exceptional, rendering flashlights of little importance.

The most important changes I have found personally have been in myself, and I praise the Lord for that. During my years at San Quentin I came to view the inmates as God's creations who had gone astray. I came to understand that they needed my guidance rather than my judgment. There were times, of course, when they tested my patience, as it isn't always easy to try to pick up broken pieces; in fact, sometimes it is impossible because some inmates simply don't want to turn their lives around. They just want to excuse their behavior and/or blame it on others, and hope for a loophole to get them out of prison so they can return to the very lifestyle that got them there in the first place. But for those who are willing to let God's Spirit work in them, anything is possible. On my own part I had to learn patience and humility, and working as I did kept me in prayer, oftentimes for tolerance.

One of my greatest challenges was working with inmates who were involved in homosexual activities. I use the word activity because many of the men were not homosexuals; they were simply engaging in the behavior because they believed they had a right to satisfy their sexual appetites, and while in prison there were no alternatives.

Inmate marriages were common knowledge among the inmate population, and there were many killings and assaults related to those relationships. I am sorry to say we have individual psychiatrists who have condoned these behaviors by inmates, particularly as society moves in the direction of considering such behavior normal. As a Christian and a human being, I cannot personally condone what the Bible condemns as shameful and unnatural.

One inmate in his early twenties was married to a very attractive young woman who visited him regularly, bringing their two children along as well. Each morning this inmate would come to his assignment at the furniture factory in the company of another inmate, also assigned to the industry area. As they parted to go to their individual assignment, they kissed.

I was informed by another source of this very involved affair that did not stop within the confines of San Quentin. An outside contact was made with the young wife, instructing her to obtain a divorce so her marriage would not interfere with this homosexual relationship. In my opinion this was clearly a case of an inmate taking advantage of the prison situation and what it could offer.

The wife called my office and told me of the demand for a divorce and said that, as a wife and mother, she was very concerned about the situation. However, as a counselor I was unable to intervene on her behalf, as any discussion of these relationships had to be initiated by the inmate. Sadly I never knew how this situation ultimately turned out, but my request and recommendation to move one of the two inmates involved to another institution was accomplished. The move was swift and without complications, and I was content that it was as God willed it.

Since the late 1960s there have been radical changes in the Department of Corrections, as well as in the California State Government itself. The "lame duck" decisions by Governor Pat Brown, Sr., prior to his leaving office indicated his complete change of philosophy and attitude toward the death penalty, most of which seems to have occurred during the Caryl Chessman era. Pat Brown was the California Attorney General at the time of the prosecution of Chessman. Mr. Brown claimed his feelings at that time were part of his job, as well as his responsibility to the people of California. When he became governor, his position changed. Abolition of capital punishment came from his era.

Good prison reform was on the downslide. Lengthy appeals by those sentenced to death, a change from the previous one automatic appeal with new evidence, had been stretched to the excess of twelve years on Death Row, as inmates' rights came to the forefront and their focus became finding loopholes to get out of their sentences. This was true throughout the prison, not just on Death Row.

One inmate was deeply involved in gang warfare. He was found to be involved in supplying weapons while in the Adjustment Center. Therefore, transfer consideration to another institution for his protection was temporarily set aside, pending the investigation of the weapons situation. During the time of approximately three weeks this inmate was attacked by a high-ranking member of the Aryan Brothers. Both of the inmates were armed at the time. The attacked inmate was killed, and the District Attorney declined to prosecute the slayer, calling the murder "self-defense."

The family of the victim, with the help of a radical young attorney, filed suit against me and other California Department of Corrections staff, claiming the victim was killed because of the action taken by the staff of San Quentin in delaying recommendations for transfer so there could be an investigation of a felony act. The second part of the lawsuit referred to me and other Department of Corrections staff, claiming we conspired together maliciously and willfully to do physical injury or to have the victim killed by placing him among known murderous inmates on April 12, 1975.

A handwritten hit list was one of our primary reasons for making a search of the Adjustment Center, which led to the finding of seventeen prison-made stabbing instruments in one day. The list noted the hits to be carried out, all of which were upon Aryan Brothers or Mexican Mafia associates or sympathizers. The victim was listed as the sleeper host. Also, the victim never denied his part in that activity, or with the gang in general.

After I retired from San Quentin, a $1,250,000 lawsuit was filed against me. Former Governor Deukmajian was the Attorney General at the time, and he was most helpful, personally advising me each evening during the one week of court hearings. Then, on a Thursday night, the call came. "Joe, the plaintiff has dropped the State of California and Warden Nelson from their suit. They are going after Joe Hare, the counselor in charge of the Adjustment Center."

The next morning, as Pat and I had our devotion time, my prayer was, "Lord, you can do all things." As I left for Marin County Court, the Lord ministered to me in many ways. I prayed, "Lord, I don't even know what to ask." Then God surrounded me with His presence, and I was at peace.

When I arrived at the courthouse I said, "Here I am, Lord."

His response came so clearly: "Have no fear, for I will put words in your mouth."

When the plaintiff's attorney began to speak, continuing on for quite some time, the judge finally said to him, "I have listened to you for one week, but you have showed me no evidence to support your charge against Mr. Hare. I will give you ten minutes until lunchtime, and then I am dismissing this case." Almost immediately he hit the desk with his gavel and said, "Case dismissed."

"Thank You, Lord," I prayed.

The mother of the deceased inmate was sitting near her attorney, and I knew I needed to go to her. As the court cleared out, I found myself standing beside her. Suddenly I held my arms out to her, and she responded. As I held and comforted her, I said, "I'm sorry. Your son was not all bad. He wanted to help himself, and I tried too." I believe those were the words God had promised to put in my mouth, because a special sense of peace passed between us at that moment, this mother who had lost her son and the counselor who had been unable to prevent that loss.

Another young man had been locked up in B Section on suspicion of assault within the institution. As I passed by his cell one day, I stopped and stepped back, thinking he had spoken to me. We soon were involved in a conversation about the possibility of his returning to the general population. He told me of his fears and how the walls of his cell had only recently ceased to move in and out on him.

It seems this young man was a product of the late Timothy O'Leary, the LSD king of California. This powerful hallucinogenic drug had been like daily bread to him, as he sought hallucinations to escape the past and to imagine a future under the cloak of religion led by Mr. O'Leary. This inmate was highly intelligent and wanted to write a book that might help prevent others from being drawn into the hell he had experienced.

Timothy O'Leary twisted and used the Bible to further his own interests. Young people honored him and considered him their leader; some even thought of him as a god. This inmate and former O'Leary disciple had begun to seek the true God and had found Him in the

Holy Scriptures. He was able to enroll in a Bible study by listening to a radio program as he sat in his cell. Combined with prayer, this study revealed the truth to this inmate and set him free from the bonds of Satan and his servant Timothy O'Leary, who by this time had been released from incarceration and was back in society poisoning other young and impressionable minds. Many of these O'Leary devotees ended up destroyed in body, mind, and spirit, and some spent the remainder of their lives in prison.

Our news media made a big show for O'Leary as he was released from a minimum security institution of the California Department of Corrections, even though he had previously escaped from that institution and was gone for a considerable time. He was returned on a new charge of marijuana possession. The quantity of marijuana was great, but the sentence was light, not equaling the offense. O'Leary was released, and his death was eventually covered on television, where he was pictured as a highly intelligent contributor to society. This was a clear example of how society's negative changes impacted the penal system, particularly in California.

A former ranking member of the Black Panthers was convicted by a jury on murder, first degree. After he had served twenty-seven years, a judge acted on one of the inmate's appeals—not on new evidence but on a technicality. A key witness for the prosecution was a former informant for the FBI, but this was not disclosed during the trial. The judge used that oversight to order a new trial, setting this convicted murderer free on bail, despite the fact that he continued to cause serious problems and was violent throughout his twenty-seven years of incarceration.

San Quentin has often been a place of hatred and violence, particularly between the black and white races. The retaliation by gang affiliation adds to an aggressive hatred among the prison population. The staff no longer has the power or the right to segregate an inmate from his gang affiliations, and this exacerbates the problem, bringing about considerable destruction of a classification system that operated successfully for years. Today's system is strictly limited to the sensitivity and control of the prison gangs.

Prisons, especially maximum security facilities like San Quentin, are abnormal, in that they exist to punish, control, and hopefully rehabilitate people who have committed crimes against society. Individuals are removed from normal lifestyles and placed in these confined circumstances, separating them from family and friends and causing pain to all those involved.

Prison reform can be most helpful, but at times it can also be harmful, preventing true rehabilitation of inmates. For prison reform to be positive, it must be subject to the laws, and it must work to help the inmates understand that their crimes are subject to punishment as well as rehabilitation, rather than just helping them find a way to "beat the rap."

Christians working with inmates must help them recognize their wrongdoing and encourage them to change their behavior so they can move on to productive lives. One city official, who was a strong Christian, told me how he had joined with other church members and made regular visits to the California Medical Facility at Vacaville. This man and his family befriended one inmate and visited him often. They corresponded with him regularly, and even gave him an electric typewriter. Everyone felt good about the relationship until the inmate said he thought they were using him and he wanted compensation. This broke the relationship and deeply hurt the family, who dropped out of prison ministry entirely. Though their feelings were understandable, it is wrong to allow one bad experience to stop us from ministering God's Word to those who need it so desperately.

My dear wife has always claimed her concerns were not about my working in a prison, but rather about my 120-mile daily commutes. As I've said before, Pat has always been my listening ear and the one who encouraged me when I was depressed or discouraged. And she has prayed for the inmates faithfully.

My church friends have also shown their loving concern for me each time they heard of trouble at San Quentin. Many of these same friends extended their love and concern to the inmates of San Quentin, praying for them, visiting with them, and encouraging them, while in no way condoning or excusing their criminal acts. They believe, as I do, that when someone commits a crime, there is a need for swift, firm justice. The Bible instructs us to abide by the laws, for we cannot live peaceably without them. The Bible also tells us that if we live by God's laws, we will have no reason to fear the laws of mankind.

I personally believe our society has stretched the laws to the point that justice itself has become twisted. In fact, for the most part, the criminal element thinks of justice only as it relates to their complete acquittal. I am sorry to say that some of our district attorneys and courts have contributed to these misconceptions under their interpretation of constitutional rights. It appears to me that the Miranda Rights (the right to remain silent and to have legal counsel when being questioned by the police) are used as a technicality for the criminal to escape punishment.

Our changing times seem to coincide with our changing society. The felon in the late twentieth and early twenty-first century has changed from the older to the younger man. He is often militant or revolutionary, with no desire or intention of accepting guidance or correction. He usually considers violence on his part to be justified.

Facing reality may make him face the truth, but he resists doing that because it might prevent his acquittal.

My approach to this is that "confession is good for the soul, for running water washes clean." Roman Catholics can understand this concept by thinking of how clean they feel after honestly confessing their sins. However, before honest confession can happen, there has to be repentance, a turning away from wrong behavior and a turning toward God and His laws for mankind. That feeling of truly being scrubbed clean can only come from God, not from lying or trying to "beat the rap" through a technicality and a smart attorney. To honestly say, "I've done wrong and I'm sorry," is to take the first steps toward rehabilitation.

I recall one interview I had with a young fellow named Manuel who actually requested that I pray for him. We had discussed his crime and narcotic habit, and he seemed to realize he was at the end of the road with no way to turn. Even if the Adult Authority gave him a parole, he still had his heroin addiction to deal with, for he knew he was hooked. Manuel explained that his entire focus over the past years in prison was to convince his counselor and then the Adult Authority that narcotics no longer had a hold on him and that he had not used drugs since he had been incarcerated. He felt this would be a great asset to him in regaining his freedom.

Sadly, though, drugs are readily available in prison, and most addicts, including Manuel, continue to use narcotics even after they are incarcerated. Though it is difficult to imagine how the drug trade can continue under such tight security as is found at San Quentin and other prisons, I assure you that it does. Carriers of drugs in and out of prison range from the inmates' family members, attorneys, and even prison personnel, whether they do so out of fear and coercion, or bribery.

My interview with Manuel soon directed him to God, who is most likely to be called upon when nothing else is left. I was able to tell Manuel of another young narcotic addict who was completely released from his addiction. I told him how Jesus died not only for me, but for the drug addict as well. When the Bible says that by Jesus' stripes (or wounds) we are healed, that means body, mind, and spirit.

Manuel looked at me as I spoke, and he had tears in his eyes. "What do I have to do, Mr. Hare, to have what you have?"

I told him that God had something even more personal that was for him alone. Manuel asked me to pray for him. Oh, how the Spirit of God rejoiced! The power of God moved as we sat in my office and I held this young man's hands. I asked Manuel if he wanted to surrender his life to Jesus, and he said yes. I prayed the sinner's prayer, which basically is, "Forgive me, Lord." Manuel repeated the prayer and accepted Christ as his Savior. The change in his life was positive from that point on. Though I have lost touch with Manuel over the years, I pray he is now a strong, mature man in Christ's service.

Another inmate with whom I worked over a period of years had a somewhat similar problem, though his situation was quite different from Manuel's. Red was assigned to the Special Design Department of the San Quentin furniture factory, under my supervision. He was thirty-eight years old, and much of his life had been spent in farm labor. He had three daughters, and his wife had divorced him following the first of his three prison commitments. She later died of cancer.

Red had a problem with alcohol, which finally led to his serving three terms for attempted rapes, each of which was a nearly identical crime. Each of the three times Red went to a bar, met a woman, drank for a while, and then ended up in his female companion's room. Apparently he then became forceful in his demands and possibly his actions as well. This led to charges for a parole violation, which in itself prohibited use of alcohol. Red served an overall time of approximately twelve years.

I liked Red, and he was very open to counseling. He was a good worker, and I eventually placed him as the lead man of special design. Red was faithful to me as his supervisor, and he did a good job of directing the other inmates in my shop. Red looked much older than his thirty-eight years, and he seldom smiled or made any small talk.

During my lunch periods, Red would usually return early just to sit down and talk with me. Soon I was able to tell Red about my God and how He could also be his God. I explained to Red that God did not consider the master any greater than his servants, meaning that God saw Red and me as equals. Red soon began attending my Yokefellow groups and made good progress, which I counted a privilege to observe.

After knowing Red for a while, I was able to call him by his given name of LeRoy. Red was a name he had picked up over the years, but by the time I knew him his formerly thick red hair had thinned out and his skin was no longer as ruddy from being outside doing farm work. His friendly attitude permitted me a chance to witness to him of God's love and to share my testimony. LeRoy felt comfortable enough with me that he brought family letters and shared his problems with me, mostly about his three daughters who had been placed in separate foster homes. I often wonder what happened to LeRoy and his daughters, who suffered as a result of LeRoy's crimes and the breakup of their family.

LeRoy's case is only one of many that stems from alcohol problems, as well as drugs and illicit sex. So much of the crime in our nation today is driven by these very factors.

The weakness of the flesh has destroyed many human beings. It is difficult even to imagine a family man of good social standing being enticed to seduce and even rape a young child, sometimes his own. And yet I know it happens, for there were times I had to call upon the Lord to help me as I counseled with those who had committed such heinous crimes that it was beyond my own human ability to understand. Even then, however, I knew it was God's desire for me to counsel and help these men in such a way that they would face up to their sin and seek forgiveness.

The child molester has a rough road to walk in prison, as most inmates consider that crime as being worse than their own. Protective custody is often the only choice for those who have molested and raped babies and young children. Some of these inmates become paranoid and endeavor to rationalize or even deny their crimes, while others actually blame their young victims for "leading them on" and enticing them into something they really didn't want to do, whether the victim was a complete stranger or the perpetrator's own child.

I have found that so long as the individual is unwilling to seek forgiveness, there is little that counselors or anyone else can do but wait—and pray. Receiving understanding and patience from others can sometimes be just what's needed to nudge the offenders to admit their crimes and ask for forgiveness.

Child molestation is, of course, one of the most detestable of crimes. As a counselor I have found a great percentage of these offenses are committed by individuals with warped personalities, which makes relating to them extremely difficult. It was hard for me not to form an opinion about an inmate just by seeing the word "child molesting" or "incest" on their records.

Many of these offenses are related to a stepfather situation, or even to an unmarried couple who team up to try to rationalize their behavior by calling their illegal relationship a "common law marriage." Many of these instances of child molestation by a stepfather have been known by the mother and yet ignored because she didn't want to lose her male partner.

As a Christian my concerns for high morals as a parent are a must. I also find that our laws were meant to protect children—and that's as it should be. Time, in and of itself, is not the answer to curing or changing someone who has been involved in molesting children. For many of these perpetrators, however, that's all they get. There may be a requirement of clinical therapy, but even therapy combined with time isn't necessarily enough. Inmates who have been convicted of these despicable crimes against children must realize they have done wrong and truly want to change. This, again, starts with confession and words of repentance, but complete healing even after that takes time and discipline and counseling.

I once worked with a man in his fifties named Ron. His son ran a preschool in a very exclusive location. In his free time Ron enjoyed working part time in the preschool. He became involved in molesting several of the young children, and the son lost his license and his business. Ron lost his wife and his family. The tiny victims lost their innocence. As a parole requirement Ron was involved in therapy during the years he spent in prison, and his release had many restrictions related to his immediate family. When he was discharged he claimed he had "served his time." He was somewhat bitter when he talked of laws relating to child molesters being harassed, and he showed no concern for the young victims. He exhibited a sense of anger for what the authorities and the prison had done to him, and so I worried about what would happen once he was released. I did hear that he was attending church on a regular basis, and I have always prayed that the Holy Spirit would touch him and turn him to receive Jesus Christ as his Lord and Savior.

Another young man came to my office one day and said, "Mr. Hare, you know I have a parole date. You also know I'm an addict. I'm scared, because there's no way I can make it. You have to help me."

Can you imagine my feelings? This fellow had spent the greater part of his adult life in prison because of his addiction. Now he had a parole date and he wanted help. What could I do? How could I help someone who was an admitted drug addict?

That evening after I got home from work, I couldn't stop thinking about that young man. Suddenly I realized it was more than a concern I was feeling; it was an urging from the Lord. I talked it over with Pat and was even more certain that God was speaking to me to help this inmate. But how?

The next few days brought little direction. Then the inmate again requested to speak with me. When he arrived in my office, I told him we would start a group for addicts, no more than twelve, and for him to get them together. Within the next week we had twelve inmates and some hard-core addicts, and we began meeting together and talking over the needs of the men in the group. All were in agreement that the narcotic use must stop, but no one seemed to know how to make that happen. We hashed over many ideas, and then I sensed the Lord was ready. Future plans and ideas were flowing freely as I attempted to introduce these men to a Counselor with a healing formula that could not possibly fail. There was no attempt to turn our group into

Joe Hare with Kathi Macias

a Bible study or prayer meeting, but rather into a group that used therapy based on the promises of God.

The introductions were interesting. One young man named John had been an addict for fifteen years. It all started when John, who was from a broken family, dropped out of school. He lied about his age and joined the Merchant Marines. His first voyage was a rough one. After a few days at sea, John was very sick and there was little anyone could do to help him. Then an older deck hand gave John some "medicine" that seemed to be the answer for his remaining days at sea.

Then came his first foreign port. John went with his companion, who was older and much more experienced, to find the necessary medicine for the return trip. They made the illegal connection and returned to ship. John was now taking this medicine even when the sea wasn't rough and he wasn't sick. That's when he realized he was hooked, but he wasn't worried as there seemed to be an abundant supply.

One day there was a storm blowing. John and his friend were on deck, battening down the equipment and hatches. John's friend dropped a bottle, which broke on the steel deck. The rough seas did the rest. The abundant supply was gone. After a few days John was truly sick, and not from the rise and fall of the ocean. The voyage was a long and miserable one, as John experienced the pain of withdrawal.

Not long after his return to the United States John was arrested for possession of drugs. Probation was then, and still is now, the usual treatment for first-time offenders. However, John was soon arrested for burglary, then robbery, for which he received his sentence at San Quentin. This part of his life took place over a period of fifteen years. Now John was ready to get help.

The group was completely in the hands of my God. At each opportunity I gave these men a scripture and a promise from the Bible. My prayers for them were fervent.

As time passed I found myself questioning God because I didn't see any progress. But then I wondered just what progress I expected to see. I realized I had no idea, and we were well into the twelve-month trial period we had set for evaluation. My greatest concern was John because of his upcoming parole date. It may have been that my uneasiness about John's situation was causing me to doubt. Then I was drawn back to my Lord, for He had no place for His servant spreading doubt. In my weakness came His strength.

Before I realized what was happening, these men were no longer talking of drugs and boosting their own egos; they were talking of the future and looking forward to parole. They were asking where to find the words of promise and love I had given them. God's Word had been introduced to them, and they were now His companions. Second Corinthians 6:1-13 speaks of love and trust, and that's what was happening in this group. It was the first such group for narcotic addicts at San Quentin, as addicts had always been considered lost causes. But by God's grace these men were introduced to the One who gave them more than the will to pull themselves up by the bootstraps. He took the hand of each one personally and pulled them up Himself.

I have received only one letter from John since he was paroled, but in it he claimed to be living clean, holding down a job, and making plans for the future. A few of the others who were in the group have also contacted me, and none, to my knowledge, has ever returned to prison.

Our group was the only one of its kind at San Quentin, and we had something that must have helped these inmates. There were no drop-outs from the group, and each of these men continued to seek a better life. As far as I could see, the Bible was their source in this search. Following is a letter I received from one of the men who attended that group.

> *Dear Mr. Hare and Gang:*
>
> *I am sorry I haven't written this letter sooner but I have been working seven days a week and haven't had time to get to town to get stamps.*
>
> *Well, Mr. Hare, everything is fine here, and I am doing fine. I think of the Yokefellow gang often. Tell them hello for me, and thank them also for their prayers because I know they are praying for me. Everything here is just fine. I don't have to report each month to my parole officer or anything. I have my own little house and my own pick-up and everything. So, Mr. Hare, I know you are all praying for me. Tell Marion I am going to write his mother soon now, and tell my buddy F. that I don't think there is a tide in Clear Lake, CA.*
>
> *Well, Mr. Hare, how's your family doing? Just fine, I hope. Tell them all hello for me, and I thank them very much for sharing you with us in the Yoke Fellow class, for I got more out of it than I did anything else. Thanks again, and may God be with all of you. Please answer soon, Mr. Hare, and if you are too busy, have your wife write. I will appreciate it very much.*
>
> *Bye for now. I will never forget you.*
>
> *Bud*

Yokefellow Prison Ministry was one of many tools God used to change lives, including that of a three-time loser named Larry Baulch. As I mentioned earlier, the Reverend Cecil Osborne was instrumental in Larry's turnaround. Reverend Osborne met Larry at San Quentin and introduced him to Yokefellows. Larry soon accepted Jesus Christ, and was eventually paroled to the Palo Alto area of California. His parole hearing was favorable and he was given a release on job approval. Reverend Osborne and his church offered Larry a job as church custodian. Soon the church offered to assist him in going to seminary. He was graduated and ordained as the Reverend Larry Baulch, and authored a book titled *Return to the World.* He stayed very busy with the Yokefellow ministry, giving back where he had received. The Palo Alto area was receptive to Larry and his work, even establishing a Christian Coffee House, then a halfway house for paroled inmates.

Larry earned the trust and respect of the staff at San Quentin and other California prisons as well. He married a fine Christian woman, and they became one in the Lord. He gave his life to ministering to those in prison, though he died at a young age from cancer.

The Reverend Larry Baulch is just one of many examples of how a life can truly be changed for the better when someone is willing to face his crimes, turn from them, and give his life over to God. Those are the changes that truly rehabilitate.

> *"And this is the will of Him who sent Me, that everyone who sees the Son and believes in Him may have everlasting life; and I will raise him up at the last day" (John 6:40).*

Chapter 8

"A Man Named Odd"

In 1927 Odd Cornell was sentenced to hang for the murder of his wife and her thirteen-year-old daughter. At the time of the double murder, Odd had been a young, hardworking truck driver who believed he had finally met the woman of his dreams. He married her earlier that year and set out to build a life for them and her young daughter.

Odd's job as a truck driver often kept him on the road for several days at a time. But he didn't mind because he knew that at the end of the long haul, he would be returning home to his new family. One day, not long after the wedding, Odd came back early. What he found when he got there was not at all what he had expected—his wife was in bed with another man.

Infuriated, Odd grabbed the man and they began to fight. Hysterical, Odd's wife called the police. Before they could arrive, Odd turned the man loose and ran from the scene. His wife, however, insisted on filing charges against Odd.

The next day, after he had cooled off a bit, Odd decided to go home and try to talk to his wife. On the off chance that the man might still be there, Odd foolishly tucked a gun inside his waistband. Although the man was not at the house when Odd arrived, the betrayed husband and his defensive wife were soon exchanging angry words. As the argument escalated, Odd pulled out his gun and fired. His wife fell to the floor, her life ended in a fit of passion.

Almost immediately Odd's thirteen-year-old stepdaughter arrived home from school. When she saw her mother lying on the floor in a pool of blood, she began to scream. Panicking, Odd once again fired his gun, and soon there were two dead bodies lying on the floor in front of him. At that point Odd turned the gun on himself, inflicting a wound that nearly cost him his life. After a lengthy recovery, Odd claimed to have no memory of having shot himself, nor did he ever admit to remembering that part of the incident.

When he was charged with double murder, however, Odd never attempted to fight the charges. After a brief trial he was sentenced to death. The death sentence itself wasn't so much what scared Odd— it was what would happen to him after he died. He was, in fact, tormented with this fear as he awaited the carrying out of his death sentence, as were many of the Death Row inmates I came to know at San Quentin.

When I first met Odd, he told me his fear of what would happen to him after he was put to death was so great he had decided to try and convince everyone he was crazy. Already on Death Row, he would crawl under his bed and bark like a dog when the officers came near him. Apparently his behavior was so convincing that word of it reached the prison authorities, and the psychiatric staff soon recommended that Odd be transferred to the Mendocino State Hospital for observation. Within six weeks, however, Odd was back on the row at San Quentin.

As Odd's fear of his fate after death escalated, so did his bizarre behavior. In 1928, just prior to the setting of his execution date, then California Governor Rolf commuted Odd's death sentence to life without the possibility of parole. The governor was careful to put the commuting of Odd's sentence in a legal form that he hoped would prevent any future court or governor from changing the sentence to parole. In all, Odd spent only four months on Death Row before his sentence was commuted.

Years later the man who had been named Odd when he was born and whose strange behavior while on the row had come to typify his name said to me, "You know, Mr. Hare, I must have done a good act at being crazy. But I'm still afraid to die."

That particular conversation has stayed with me over the years. Odd and I were able to talk about many things that day, including my own belief in God and what would happen to me when I die. Odd listened politely as he always did, but did not take our discussion to the next level of accepting my faith as his own. As a result, though I often saw Odd smile and, at times, behave in a humorous manner, I seldom saw him exhibit any real joy. His fear of dying was just too great. Of course, because of San Quentin's unwritten law that no employee was allowed to pursue the subject of religion with an inmate beyond that which was initiated by the inmate himself, I was not able to bring the conversation to a personal level with Odd. The man seemed to enjoy hearing what God had done for me in my life, and he even added at one point, "I would like to know your God, Mr. Hare," but that's as far as we ever got when it came to discussing Odd's own relationship with God.

In Odd's early years at San Quentin, soon after his death sentence was commuted, he was assigned to the blacksmith shop, just beyond the outside walls of the prison, where he learned to shoe the horses owned and used by the correctional officers. He soon became an expert in the skill of horseshoeing. Even though he had no chance at parole, it was obvious he wanted to learn a skilled trade. After his five-year stint at the blacksmith shop, he worked for fifteen years in the prison shoe shop, quickly mastering the trade of making and repairing shoes. Later he went into the machine shop for another fifteen years, and was soon respected as one of the best machinists in the entire prison. In addition, during the years I oversaw the work done in San Quentin's furniture factory, Odd would drop by to visit the shop. He seemed to enjoy watching the rough hardwood turned into custom pieces of furniture, and he was proud of the work done by the other inmates. Overall, Odd was an easy guy to work and get along with. In all of his years at San Quentin, I was never aware of his having even one disciplinary infraction.

In spite of the fact that he would talk to me on occasion, however, Odd had very little to say to anyone else. He was not much for socializing, and he never left himself open to being approached by other inmates. Although he was a relatively small man, he was stocky and strong in appearance. His solemn look and his reputation for having had his sentence commuted due to his strange behavior was enough to keep others from pushing him too far. In fact, in his younger days at San Quentin, Odd was part of the boxing team and seemed quite proud of that accomplishment. In spite of his reticence to talk, he did enjoy relating tales about his life, though it was apparent as the years progressed that San Quentin was the only life Odd knew or cared about.

Through the years, as my position at San Quentin changed from correctional officer to Adjustment Center counselor, Odd and I kept in touch. Due to his tenure and good behavior, he basically had an "open ticket" to visit most places inside the confines of San Quentin. Because he considered me a friend, he came to see me periodically wherever I might be working, though he never abused or took advantage of our friendship.

When I first became a correctional counselor, Odd was on my caseload in the West Block. I studied his case history and his criminal potential in preparation for counseling with him. He was getting up there in years and I felt his future criminal potential was almost nonexistent, but the clause in his commuted sentence was strong:

"without possible parole." Even though I thought Odd could make it on the outside and not be a danger to society, I didn't see any way of getting past that ironclad clause in his sentence. Besides, Odd had no family or friends outside the prison walls. Still, the thought that he had long since paid his debt to society and could function in the real world continued to nag at me, and I spent much time in prayer on the subject.

One day in 1968, as Odd and I were talking, out of the blue I asked him, "Odd, do you ever have the desire for release?"

"I never think about release, Mr. Hare," Odd answered matter-of-factly.

I have no idea why I asked him that question, because I knew a release was next to impossible, unless the current governor could find a way to intervene, and that was highly unlikely. After hearing Odd's response and realizing that the commute sentence had taken away any hope he might have for a better tomorrow, I dropped the subject—no sense stirring up something that just couldn't happen.

Then one evening not long after our conversation, while I was on my way home from work, I stopped at the Franklin Canyon Dairy, where Pat and I purchased our fresh dairy products each week. I had gotten to know the owners, the Zupon family, over the years, and as I started talking with Mr. Zupon I told him about Odd. It was obvious to me that Mr. Zupon was interested in Odd's situation, so I asked him if he would consider helping the man out by giving him a job and a place to live on his ranch. Mr. Zupon agreed to think it over, and I left wondering why in the world I had even brought up the subject, since there was little or no chance of obtaining a release for Odd. Still, I had felt compelled to try.

The following week Mr. Zupon asked if he could meet Odd. I told him I would check into arranging a meeting. As I drove home from the dairy farm that evening, my mind was swirling with thoughts. I asked myself why I was pursuing such a hopeless situation, as I had no idea how I would ever pull off such a feat as getting Odd released from prison. "What now, Lord?" I prayed, as I continued to consider the possibilities.

Within days I found myself talking with Warden Louis Nelson. As I poured out my feelings and thoughts concerning Odd, the warden listened intently, and then said, "A big job, Joe." Those were his only words, and then we parted.

But the conversation had apparently had an effect on Warden Nelson, because the wheels of bureaucracy began to turn. First came the Adult Authority hearings, and then a letter arrived from Governor Pat Brown, commuting Odd Cornell's sentence by lifting the "no parole" clause. This in itself was nothing short of a miracle, considering how carefully the former governor had worded Odd's commute. After that came the board date, when Odd Cornell would go before the parole board for his verdict. The results? "Release upon program approval."

When the approval for release came through, I'm not sure who was more excited—Odd or me! This was 1973, however, and much had changed since Odd had last lived as a free man. He was understandably frightened at the idea of once again living outside the prison walls after forty-six years of incarceration.

The first thing I did after receiving word of the approval of Odd's release was to set up an appointment for him to meet with the eldest son of Odd's perspective employer, Mr. Zupon. John Zupon came to the prison, and I took him back to the cellblock to Odd's cell—his "house," as the old inmate called it. The meeting went well, and it was soon agreed that upon Odd's release, he would go to live and work on the Zupons' dairy farm.

I was thrilled, to say the least, and yet I had my doubts. I wondered how the public would react to this man's release from prison. I knew the press could blow the whole thing if the story were presented in the wrong way. So I called Dave Hendricks, a Christian friend of mine and editor of a popular local newspaper called the *Contra Costa Times*. I knew Dave well enough to know that he would be gracious in the handling and writing of Odd's story.

On the day of Odd's release, the warden and I decided it would be best if we drove him to his new home ourselves. It was quite an exciting experience, as Odd had been locked up so long he had never seen such modern roads or vehicles. In fact, the entire outside world was new to Odd. He had never seen a grocery store, other than a small "mom and pop" establishment. Even stopping at the gas station was like a first-time event for him, as that had changed drastically from the time he was a young truck driver. This now seventy-six-year-old man, who didn't look a day over sixty, told us as we drove along that he hadn't had a good night's sleep since all these plans for a new life had begun to take shape. He had no idea what to expect, and he was understandably more than a little concerned, but the drive down the two-lane road with its view of the surrounding hills, cattle, trees, and other greenery, was relaxing to all of us.

We arrived at the ranch mid-afternoon. The weather was excellent that day, sunny, clear, and warm. The Zupon family was most gracious, as they showed Odd to his new quarters, an apartment just under the main house. There was still a bit of work to be done to the apartment, but it was quite livable as it was, and undoubtedly seemed like a mansion to a man who was used to referring to a 4.9 x 7.6-foot cell with a toilet and wash basin (cold water only!) as "home." In fact, I remember thinking that I had never seen Odd exhibit such excitement and joy, particularly as he examined the private bath and shower that was part of his new living quarters.

As Odd saw his new surroundings for the first time, several interested newspaper reporters were in attendance, including my friend Dave Hendricks from the *Contra Costa Times*. I don't remember a lot about the stories written by the other reporters, though I don't recall anything negative, but I was very pleased with the article Dave wrote.

For the first three weeks of Odd's new life, all went well. Then, suddenly, he stopped eating and didn't want to talk to anyone. Before long I'd spot him sitting on the roadside each evening, waiting for my car to pass by on my way home from work. That's when it hit me. Odd was homesick—for San Quentin!

Unfortunately I didn't get much help from Odd's parole agent in the old inmate's adjustment to his new life. He seemed to resent having Odd on his caseload. In retrospect, some of his concerns may have been valid, including Odd's advanced age, his lengthy incarceration, and the fact that he was an epileptic. In addition, Odd made no attempt to hide the fact that he thought "Mr. Hare" was the only one who could do anything right, and that was bound to create some resentment on the part of the parole agent. Soon the agent grew tired of dealing with the old man, and he even began making negative statements about Odd to the fine Zupon family who had taken him in. As a result the Zupons became fearful about having Odd around their young children.

Then, one evening, instead of spotting Odd sitting on the roadside waiting for my car to come by, I found out he had skipped supper and just walked down the long gravel driveway to the road, then left the ranch. Late that night in the city of Martinez, approximately six miles from the ranch, Odd had an epileptic seizure and was picked up by the police and retained overnight at the local hospital. In a few days his parole officer moved him from the ranch to an old rundown hotel, also located in Martinez.

With the help of the Martinez police, I managed to locate Odd on Christmas Eve, just a couple of days after he was moved to the hotel. At that time he had been out on parole only eight weeks. When I arrived at the hotel, Odd was lying in bed and was unable to look at me. "I'm sorry I let you down, Mr. Hare," were his only words of greeting. His hotel room was dirty, his face was bruised, and he was unshaven. The hotel had a common bathroom, used by the other tenants, and Odd had only a single burner hot plate in the corner of his room, where he boiled coffee. That coffee, along with some sweet rolls, seemed to be his only source of nutrition.

My heart was grieved to see him in such a condition after having had such high hopes for his new life. Impulsively I asked him if he would like to come to our home for Christmas dinner to celebrate the Lord's birthday. Odd agreed, though it was obvious he was hurt and embarrassed for me to see him in such a condition.

Odd was cleaned up and ready to go when I picked him up on Christmas day, but his mood was still somewhat somber. As I drove Odd to our home, I prayed silently, *What do you want me to do, Lord?* I felt crushed and personally responsible for Odd's situation. As the day progressed, however, the former inmate began to loosen up and join in the festivities, eventually having a wonderful time at our home in Concord. Our youngest daughter, Sharon, was home for the holidays with one of her friends from college, and we all had such a great visit. Odd never once mentioned San Quentin, but joined right in the laughter and conversation, enjoying the food and fellowship as we celebrated Christ's birth. Before he left to return to his hotel room that night, my wife fixed a huge plate of food for him to enjoy the next day. He accepted it graciously, as he did everything we did for him.

When I dropped Odd off at his hotel room that night he turned to me and asked, "Mr. Hare, why did you invite me to your home for dinner?"

I shrugged and smiled. "Maybe my God wanted it that way, Odd."

He paused and then said, "I sure would like to know this God of yours."

I have often asked myself if I should have pursued the conversation with him, and yet I know now, as I knew then, that I had said and done all God had called me to at that point. And so we parted that Christmas day.

When the holidays were over I made several calls to the Parole Department and also to the Social Welfare Office in Martinez, and before long Odd was moved out of the hotel into a house in West Pittsburgh, California, where he would live with other senior adults his age. Sadly, Odd wasn't happy there either, wanting to return to the only place he knew as home—his prison cell in San Quentin. His relationship with his parole agent had not improved, and soon Odd was accused of assaulting the lady who ran the house where he lived. Odd claimed she was taking his welfare money from his room. Whether or not that was true, I can't really say, but the incident did trigger a series of events that eventually got him sent back to prison, this time to the Men's Colony at San Luis Obispo, where he died a couple of years later.

My relationship with Odd spanned many years, and to a large degree it was unique, in that I never felt led to pursue getting someone a parole to the extent that I did for Odd. Though it seemed an impossible cause, the pieces all fell into place, and I've always believed God had His hand in the entire procedure, as there is no other explanation for the parole's being granted. Though I've often wondered about the way things turned out, I have no regrets about my part in helping Odd obtain his release from San Quentin. I did what I believed I was called to do, and the results were in God's hands. It is my firm belief that, at some point before Odd died, God honored the desire of his heart, which he had expressed to me on more than one occasion: "I sure would like to know this God of yours, Mr. Hare."

> *...that I may know Him and the power of His resurrection, and the fellowship of His sufferings, being conformed to His death, if, by any means, I may attain to the resurrection from the dead (Philippians 3:10,11).*

Conclusion

"I was in prison, and you came to me." Although I was a Christian before I began my career as a correctional officer at San Quentin, Matthew 25:36 had never meant much to me before that. Now I consider it one of my favorite scriptures in the entire Bible, because I have seen what a difference even one person can make in the lives of these inmates.

As I have said many times, I never planned to make a career out of prison work. I went into it with the idea that it was a temporary job to support my family until something better came along. The pay was low, the commute was long and tiresome, and the working shifts were a strain on my family. But I now know for certain that God led me to San Quentin in order to fulfill His purposes for my life, as well as the lives of others I was privileged to meet within those prison walls.

But it wasn't just me. So many have answered the call to minister in this tremendous mission field—some, like me, as a vocation; others, purely as volunteers.

I remember one particular occasion when I was still in my early years of employment at San Quentin and I was serving one day as part of the security squad (known as the "goon squad") during a chapel service. The inmate choir was singing, and other inmates were seated in the pews, waiting for the new chaplain, Harry Howard, to begin speaking. Suddenly a crazed inmate, carrying a homemade knife known as a "shiv," jumped up and ran toward the lectern. Before we could stop him he grabbed Harry and held him in a chokehold, with the shiv pressed to his throat. Apparently it was the inmate's intention to use the chaplain as a hostage in hopes of bargaining for his own release. However, the inmate obviously hadn't taken into account or didn't fully understand the fact that the prison has a policy of non-negotiation with inmates who have taken hostages and are trying to bargain for their own escape. (This is true even for volunteers, who must sign a form stating they understand that if they are ever taken hostage, the prison officials will not negotiate for their release if it involves the inmate's release as well.)

Another factor this inmate had not taken into account was God's intervention. As Chaplain Howard stood in the inmate's stranglehold, his breath being choked out of him, he suddenly fainted and slid to the floor. This so alarmed the inmate that he immediately dropped his weapon and surrendered. Through it all, the choir continued to sing, not missing a beat. In the years that followed, this particular chaplain became highly respected and loved by many of the inmates, as he faithfully served and ministered to them. Reverend Byron Eshelman was another chaplain who served at San Quentin for more than twenty years and was a great help to me on many occasions.

In approximately 1960, Tennessee Ernie Ford came to San Quentin to record an album with the San Quentin Chapel Choir. What a blessing that rendering of those old-time hymns of the Church proved to be in the years that followed.

And then there was Billy Graham, who was conducting a crusade at the San Francisco Cow Palace when he was invited to come and minister at San Quentin. He agreed, and when he showed up on the afternoon of May 16, 1958, he found more than 4,000 inmates sprawled out in the hot sunshine of the baseball field, anxiously waiting to hear him speak. The renowned Baptist preacher immediately established a rapport with his listeners when he jokingly invited them to "attend the crusade meeting tonight at the Cow Palace—if you can make it." It was obvious his audience appreciated his humor, as they laughed and relaxed, visibly attentive to his words. "God will forgive," Graham told the men. "Regardless of how black your crime, God will forgive you. You can live a Christian life here and now—for God will go with you."

As the service drew to a close, 623 of those 4,000-plus inmates in attendance came forward to accept the Rev. Graham's invitation to receive Jesus as Lord and Savior and to "live for God in prison," repeating this prayer after him: "Oh, God, I'm a sinner. I'm sorry for my sins. I receive Christ as my Savior. I confess Him as Lord from this moment on. I'm going to live for Him and follow Him and serve Him."

A spokesman for the Graham team later said it was the largest percentage ever to respond at an evangelistic service anywhere. As Rev. Graham said, "It takes great courage for men to step out and witness for God in these surroundings."

When the service was over, hundreds of inmates crowded around Rev. Graham, talking and joking with him, and asking for autographs. Later, though he still had a crusade to conduct at the Cow Palace that evening, the evangelist took the time to visit Death Row, speaking to eighteen of its then twenty-one inmates. The famous Caryl Chessman was one of the three inmates who chose not to meet with Graham.

The most exciting thing to me, however, was seeing the effects of Rev. Graham's visit long after he left. Chaplain James Robinson of *His Way Ministry* in Concord, California, asked me what was being done in the way of follow-up ministry at San Quentin. As we discussed this great need, this kind and generous man of God offered 3,000 Bibles for the inmates. They arrived the next day, and within two weeks not one Bible was left unclaimed. The inmates had new reading material! In addition, I was happy to see that the recently constructed religious center had become a hubbub of activity. Bible studies flourished, many led by volunteers from the outside.

Then, on October 25, 1975, San Quentin held a "Jesus Celebration." The event was held on a Saturday and had to compete with foul weather, the showing of an unusually popular movie to the residents of the East Block and the D Section from the South Block, not to mention that most inmates valued their time in the yard on Saturday mornings. And yet the event was successful, with a good turnout for the five hours of inspiration and entertainment, which included various singers and gospel groups, such as Crusaders for Christ, who opened the show.

Several of the event's participants also shared their testimonies about how God had changed their lives. One of those giving his testimony was Clarence "Light Bulb" McDowell, a former Death Row resident, who stated emphatically that ever since he had come to accept and know Jesus Christ as his Savior he had found a peace that he had never before imagined. Then Steve Pierce took the stage, explaining that he was a former San Quentin "con" who had lived a life of crime for years and then spent many more years walking the prison yard and wondering what had gone so wrong in his life. Then he met Jesus Christ and found a joy and purpose he never knew existed.

Joe Sobrano, another former inmate and by then a part of the Teen Challenge ministry, got up and told how he had been raised in Hoyo Mara in East Los Angeles, where he had gotten involved in crime at a very early age. He had years of experience as a member of the drug world, which had resulted in numerous arrests and trips to the California Department of Corrections. In fact, Joe had first met his father while both were serving time in the California Training Facility in Soledad. But all that changed when Joe received Jesus as Savior. No longer did he live in fear of the police, because he was no longer transporting drugs. The only thing he carried with him anymore was his love for Jesus Christ—and he was more than anxious to pass that on to anyone who was interested.

Athletes in Action was the next group to get up and talk about their love for Jesus. These men were all well known athletes, and the inmates seemed impressed that such physically strong men were not ashamed to declare their love for Jesus Christ.

And then came Mr. Pat Boone, who had flown in from Phoenix for his first opportunity to meet the San Quentin residents en masse. He had been to other prisons and had limited experience with the California Department of Corrections, but he had not performed or ministered at San Quentin prior to that day.

After a brief statement expressing his pleasure at being there, Mr. Boone created a mood of complete acceptance by performing some of his earlier, best known songs, including "Love Letters in the Sand," which was well received by everyone in attendance. He also sang several songs that had been written and/or recorded by his late father-in-law, Red Foley. Many of these, of course, were hymns of worship to God: "I Am Weak, But Thou Art Strong"; "Will the Circle Be Unbroken?"; "There Will Be Peace in the Valley"; and "No Turning Back."

Pat Boone, whose real name is Charles Eugene Boone, became a Christian at age thirteen. He began his singing career at nineteen, and for years he has been known by his trademark white bucks. When asked why he came to San Quentin, Pat replied that he believed at the end of his life he would be asked what he had done for those confined in prisons throughout the world. "I guess my motive is of a selfish nature," he answered, but then added, "It feels good to be a light in the darkness."

"I was in prison, and you came to me...."

As I finished the last chapter of this manuscript, I closed my eyes for a moment, reflecting on the many memories stirred up by my writing. When I opened my eyes I realized my hand was resting on a file. I opened it and found a handwritten note addressed to K.S.Q. I had no idea who or what K.S.Q. might be, and there was no date on the note. I decided it must have been among my personal belongings when I cleaned out my desk on my last working day in the Security Housing at San Quentin, though I didn't remember having seen the note before.

I looked at the note and realized the words were a confirmation from individuals considered to be the hard core of the California prison system, on behalf of the inmates in the Adjustment Center. As I read the note I began to bubble with joy and excitement, and then I bounded up the stairs to find my wife. "Pat, look what I found! Read it."

She did, and when she finished she looked up at me with great love shining in her eyes. "This is beautiful," she said. And then we thanked God for those simple written words, which seemed to be a final seal on my many years at San Quentin State Prison:

> *Dear K.S.Q.*
>
> *It is our understanding that Mr. Joe Hare, the head counselor in the Adjustment Center, is soon to retire. What we would like for you to do is get an interview with Mr. Hare as to what lies ahead for inmates who are pending transfer.*
>
> *(Signed)*
> *Inmates*
> *Adjustment Center*

> *P.S. If Mr. Hare is not leaving,*
> *we would still like for you to speak*
> *to him.*

> *P.P.S. Believe me, an interview*
> *with Joe Hare is one in a million!*

What an honor to read those words of admiration and respect from inmates who represented such a big part of my life! It was a confirmation to me that God had indeed placed me in prison so He could use me to help those who were paying a great price for their wrong choices and actions. I couldn't change these men, and I couldn't force them to make better and wiser decisions than they had in the past. I could, however, listen, counsel, encourage, and pray for them. Sometimes they responded well and I saw positive changes. Sometimes they didn't. Sometimes I even felt as if I'd failed. But deep down I knew the only thing I could really offer any of them was the love of Jesus right where they were—and then the choice was theirs. Sometimes they made the right choice and changed for the better... sometimes for the worse. But as George Jackson said, "Prison can make you or break you, but it leaves no man unchanged."[2]

The years I spent at San Quentin changed my life—and my heart—dramatically. God enriched me by allowing me to work there, and I was definitely changed for the better during that time. God taught me that, while it is necessary to be strong, we also must be understanding and compassionate. While we must recognize and admit our own sins and failures if ever we are to change for the better, we also must forgive and come alongside those who are trying to turn their lives around, and help them walk the path that leads to true freedom. In the words of another famous inmate—one who, unlike George Jackson, made the choice to *change for the better*—Charles

"Tex" Watson, formerly of the Charles Manson clan: "Brother, the Lord has already got me out of prison and set me free."

As He has done for me—and will do for you, if you will *choose* to let Him.

> *"For I will be merciful to their unrighteousness, and their sins and their lawless deeds I will remember no more" (Hebrews 8:13).*

Glossary of Common Prison Terms

Felony: A crime carrying a sentence of more than one year

Felon: One convicted of a felony offense

Miranda Rights: The need for someone being arrested to be told they have the right to remain silent and to have an attorney present during questioning

Cellblock: Living area in a prison

The Alley: Area between two buildings (approximately 12 x 200 feet), with shops on lower level; notorious for killings in San Quentin

Sally Port: An entrance/exit with a gate at each end, one of which remains closed when the other is open, preventing escape

Between Gates: The sally port going into the inner walls of San Quentin

Fish: New inmates or corrections officers

Goon Squad: Security team of officers used for special security or searches

Tips: Gangs

Sleeper Host: A gang member in charge of carrying out a hit

Walk-Alone Status: A security measure for certain inmates

Condemned (sentence): Condemned to death by the court

Intermediate (sentence): A sentence that has a minimum and maximum length

Adult Authority Appearance: Parole review for consideration of release

Close Security: A security classification: minimum, medium, close, maximum

Protective Custody: Protection from the general population, specifically lock-up

Disciplinary Line: Relative to a disciplinary report on an inmate

About the Authors

Born in Newark, New Jersey, to Irish immigrant parents, first-generation American **Joseph "Joe" Hare** and his three brothers and one sister grew up in a close-knit family where both parents worked to make ends meet.

Then, as America was drawn into World War II, Joe was diagnosed with a blood clot on his brain. When his medical condition worsened, he was introduced to a renowned brain specialist named Professor Purse, who not only operated successfully on Joe but also influenced him greatly throughout his life.

A few years later, in Berkeley, California, Joe married Eileen Patricia McCormick (Pat). He and Pat now have two lovely daughters, Carol and Sharon, a granddaughter named Michele, and a son-in-law named Bill, who is married to Carol and, in Joe's words, "is the son we never had."

Joe worked as a carpenter until September 1949 when God redirected his life and he soon found himself embarking on a new profession, something he would never have chosen for himself but that he has never regretted—working as a correctional officer at the California State Prison at San Quentin. While employed at the prison he went to night school and received his degree in psychology. As a result he ended up working as a counselor in the Adjustment Center of the prison, a section of the facility that housed some of its most dangerous inmates.

Since his retirement from San Quentin, Joe has worked as a licensed general building contractor. He is much in demand at churches and other venues, where he speaks of his experiences as a correctional officer at the notorious prison of San Quentin. He and Pat continue to live in Concord, California.

***

Kathi Macias is an award winning writer who has authored seventeen books. Kathi has also ghostwritten and collaborated on several others, and has published numerous articles, short stories, and poems in various periodicals. She is a staff member for a worldwide manuscript critique service, a member of The Christian PEN, CAN, CWFI, AWSA, and ACFW, and she recently won the grand prize in an international writing contest.

A former newspaper columnist and string reporter, Kathi has taught creative writing and business writing in various venues, and served as an associate pastor for six years at a large Southern California church. Kathi is a popular speaker at churches, women's clubs and retreats, and writers' conferences, and she has appeared on several radio and TV programs.

A mother and grandmother, Kathi lives in Homeland, CA, with her husband, Al, where she is currently at work on several writing and editing projects, and where she and Al spend their spare time riding their Harley.

(Endnotes)
[1] George Jackson, *Soledad Brother: The Prison Letters of George Jackson* (New York: Coward-McCann, 1970).
[2] ibid.

www.ingramcontent.com/pod-product-compliance
Lightning Source LLC
Chambersburg PA
CBHW061249280526
45784CB00002B/693